SELL SMARTER NOT HARDER

PROVEN STRATEGIES TO GET *YOUR* **PRODUCTS**

SEEN & SOLD

SAMUEL CHAPMAN

ISBN: 9798304590983
Imprint: Independently published

First Edition

Copyright © Samuel Chapman 2024. All rights reserved.

No part of this book may be reproduced, stored or transmitted by any means, except as permitted by UK copyright law or the author.

The information in this book is for general guidance only and is based on the authors experiences and research. While efforts have been made to ensure accuracy, the author accepts no responsibility for errors, omissions, or any outcomes arising from the use of this material. The author disclaims liability for any loss, or damage resulting from reliance on this content.

Thank you...

to my mum, Jackie
Thank you for your unwavering love, support, and guidance. I am forever grateful for your wisdom and encouragement.

to my sister, Georgina
Thank you for believing in me from the very beginning of this rollercoaster journey.

to my partner, Pip
Thank you for never doubting me or my ideas. Your faith in me and your willingness to help turn my dreams into reality means more than words can express.

Without you, I don't know where I'd be today, but I definitely wouldn't be here writing this book.

> This book is dedicated to any small business owner with a passion.
>
> Whether you are just starting your journey or have spent years feeling stuck and unsure.
>
> Dream big and let this book guide you to your inevitable success.

One
Introduction 1

Two
Why Did You Start Your Product Business 9

Three
Current Challenges of Product Businesses 15

Four
What it Means to Sell Smarter, Not Harder 21

Five
The 4 Pillars of a Wildly Successful Product Business 27

Six
What is Mindset Marketing? 39

Seven
Finding Your Perfect Customers 45

Eight
The Mindset Marketing Formula 63

Nine
Your Irresistible Offer 93

Ten
Products your Perfect Customer will Love 115

Eleven
The Customer Growth Journey 127

Twelve
S.E.R.V.I.C.E 141

Thirteen
Making Bold Decisions 155

About the Author 179

One

Introduction

One Introduction

Selling your products should feel exciting, not exhausting.

Yet, if you're like most product business owners you've probably felt overwhelmed by the sheer amount of effort it takes to stand out in today's competitive market.

From market stall sellers, to brick and mortar and online businesses - Everyone has to know how to stand out so that your perfect customer will buy from YOU!

There are **3 essential steps** that every prospective buyer must go through in order for you to make sales.

They need to:

- **Discover who you are**
- **Like what you do**
- **Trust in you**

And here lies the problem.

You're likely not a marketing expert.

Nor are you likely to have a full understanding of who your perfect customers are, or why they are really looking for your product.

(even if you disagree with this second statement, I have been proven right 99% of the time when I come to work with product business owners who tell me otherwise).

One *Introduction*

There are two other things I've noticed when working with product business owners:

- 1. They've spent countless hours curating or creating your products, only to see lukewarm sales.

- 2. They've posted on social media, sent out emails, and tried different marketing strategies, but feel like they're throwing spaghetti at the wall as nothing sticks, or makes the desired impact... all while watching others seemingly do it so easily!

If you can relate to either of these, I'm here to tell you there is a smarter way to get your products seen and sold.

You can reach the right customers without constantly grinding or feeling stuck in a never-ending cycle of hustling, and working more hours than you'd dare to think about.

> My question for you is, are you committed to the process of achieving the goals, success and lifestyle you want?
>
> ...or are you just interested in achieving the end result?

Here's the difference...

When you are committed to the process, you will learn what you need to do, and how to do it.

You don't allow yourself, your current skills or beliefs to hold you back.

One *Introduction*

You will rise above old thought patterns and become the Leader, the Boss and the CEO your product business needs, so it can achieve the goals and lifestyle you want.

Here's the great news, there are proven strategies the most successful product businesses use to achieve their goals faster.

With these strategies, you can:

- Make more sales

- Make more money

- Make more profits

And

- Finally live the life you want, the one you dreamed of when you first wanted to open your product business.

To have a truly successful product based business, you need to follow a particular set of steps, in the right order, at the right time.

Over the next pages I'll give you my proven step-by-step formula that I teach within the Zenith training program. This will help you attract more of the right customers (who actually want to buy), make more sales, and finally be able to take home more income from your business.

One *Introduction*

This book is designed to show you how to sell smarter, not harder. Getting your products seen and sold with ease will no longer be your nightmare... no matter what you sell, or where you sell from.

Throughout this book there will be action steps for you to take. To get the best results I encourage you to take notes as you go.

Please don't just go through the motions and hope that reading through this book will simply be enough.

You need to be fully engaged, put in the work and stay committed to achieving the results you deserve.

Hello My name is Samuel Chapman, small business owner, dog dad, effortless-sales enthusiast, and your business coach. I've spent years helping businesses like yours go from struggling to success after going through the same trials and tribulations with my own small businesses.

I am on a mission to show you that every product-based business can flourish and grow, no matter the challenges. Regardless of what you sell, or whether you have a physical or online location.

With the right knowledge, tools, and inspiration you can achieve amazing results.

Whether you're just starting out or looking to scale and grow, the principles and tools in this book will help you connect with more customers, build their trust, and ultimately sell more... without burning out.

One *Introduction*

Throughout this journey, you'll discover:

- The 4 Key Pillars for a wildly successful product business

- How to identify your perfect customers and capture their attention.

- How to create products your perfect customer will love.

- How to optimise your marketing to cut through the noise.

- The importance of trust-building in today's marketplace.

- The confidence-building strategies to make bold business decisions.

This book is not just a guide, it's a blueprint for any product business owner that wants to achieve wild success!

Let's get started and transform the way you approach sales, so you can start getting your products in front of the people who truly want and need them the most.

One *Introduction*

zenith
/ ˈzɛnɪθ /

noun
1. the time at which something is most powerful or successful.

Two

Why Did You Start Your Product Business

Two *Why Did You Start Your Product Business*

Before we begin I'd like you to take a moment to reflect on why you started your product business.

Was it just about making money, or was there something deeper?

Perhaps you wanted to bring something unique into the world - a product that fills a gap, sparks joy, or solves a problem.

Maybe it was about the freedom to create your life on your own terms, to build something meaningful from the ground up.

Or perhaps it was the desire to make an impact, to leave your mark.

Understanding your 'why' is crucial.

It's the core of your business and the fuel that keeps you going when things get tough, and let's face facts, going into business isn't all sunshine and roses. There are going to be tough days, there are going to be days where you just want to bury your head under your duvet and wish everyone and everything would disappear.

I know I'm not the only one who has been through the struggle to get their business to take off, but it's how you get back up, how you dust yourself down and how you carry on knowing that what you're out to achieve has a purpose.

Two *Why Did You Start Your Product Business*

You see, when the focus is only on the end result, i.e., selling more, making more money, and proving to yourself that you made the right decision, it's easy to lose sight of that bigger purpose.

But when you tap into your deeper reason for starting, everything else begins to make sense.

You start to see that your business isn't just about transactions; it's about creating two things:

- Genuine value for your customers

- Building a brand that resonates with people on a personal level.

Your 'why' is the foundation for everything in your business - from the products you create to the way you communicate with your customers.

It's what makes you unique in a crowded marketplace (which is SO important for you to stand out).

Understanding and reconnecting with that deeper purpose will guide you through the ups and downs of being a business owner and help you navigate the challenges that inevitably come your way.

Action Step:

Reconnecting with your 'Why'

Take a moment to really dig into the deeper reasons for starting your business.

Use the following prompts to guide your reflection:

What Inspired You to Start?

- What moment or experience first sparked the idea for your business?

- Was there a particular problem you wanted to solve or something unique you wanted to bring into the world?

What Drives You?

- Beyond money, what keeps you motivated to show up every day?

- Is it freedom, creativity, impact, or something else?

How Do You Want to Be Remembered?

- What kind of legacy do you want your business to leave behind?

- How do you want your customers to feel about your brand and what you offer?

Two *Why Did You Start Your Product Business*

How Does Your Business Reflect Your Values?

- List 3 core values that you want your business to embody.

- How do these values show up in your products and customer experience?

Now, Write a Personal Mission Statement

Using the insights from the questions above, write a one- or two-sentence mission statement for your business.

This statement should reflect your deeper "why" and guide you through every decision you make.

I will share my mission statement with you as an example of what one looks like:

> *I believe that every product-based business can flourish and grow. Regardless of what you sell, or from where, with the right knowledge, tools, and inspiration, you can achieve amazing results.*

Three

Current Challenges of Product Businesses

Three Current Challenges of Product Businesses

Running a product business today is no small feat.

The landscape is evolving at lightning speed, with new technologies, platforms, and trends shaping how businesses operate and connect with their customers, no matter how big or small they might be.

However, the core challenge remains the same, and many product businesses face it.

What I'm talking about is **visibility**.

Your perfect customer is swimming, drowning and suffocating in marketing, social media posts and sales messages.

In fact, we all are!

In today's world we are exposed to so many marketing messages everywhere we look from the moment we wake up to the moment we go to sleep. Through our in-boxes, TV, social media, websites, billboards... EVERYWHERE.

Different brands trying to get our attention literally around the clock.

And that flood of marketing is only going to continue.

In a time where you can have your business found by people on the other side of the world by putting your products on a website and starting a social media channel, you'd be fooled into thinking it was easy to be seen and sold.

Three *Current Challenges of Product Businesses*

The fact of the matter is that you are competing with thousands of new products launching every single week. This means your fantastic product will easily get lost in the noise if you're not super clear on *who* your products help and exactly *how* they help them.

Wherever you're selling from the challenge of getting noticed by the right people is real.

Compounding this is the need to build trust.

Customers today have more options than ever and convincing them to choose your product over others can feel like an uphill battle. Without the right strategy, that feeling will be a reality.

Here is what happens

Your perfect customer is filtering most marketing messages right out of their conscious thoughts. So many stimuli are bombarding the brain it isn't possible to give all of them the attention they're looking for.

However, It just takes one little message to hit them squarely on their HOT button for it to be noticed.

This is the thing that makes them stand up and pay attention to what you have to say!

It might also explain why your current, or previous marketing campaigns or social media posts have failed to deliver the kind of results you wanted.

Three Current Challenges of Product Businesses

When you put the time and effort into really understanding who your perfect customer is, what they want, need or desire the most, and how your product will give it to them, your marketing and your socials are going to...

Hit. the. BULLSEYE!

This switches on your perfect customers' HOT button and get them interested in what you have to say, and sell.

Common Pitfalls and Mistakes

There are a few common mistakes many business owners fall into, often without even realising it:

- **Focusing too much on the product**
  You may have an incredible product, but without the right marketing or customer engagement, it will never reach its full potential.

  Many business owners spend the majority of their time perfecting the product itself, without investing enough in the strategies that will actually get it seen and sold.

- **Neglecting customer experience**
  In today's market, customers expect more than just a product with average customer service. They want an _experience_.

  Businesses that fail to deliver consistent, engaging, and personal experiences often struggle with customer retention.

Three *Current Challenges of Product Businesses*

- **Not using data**
  With so much data available, it's surprising how many businesses still make decisions based on instinct alone.

  Data provides powerful insights into what's working, what isn't, and most importantly why. Failing to use these insights often leads to wasted time, effort, money and missed opportunities.

- **Inconsistent marketing**
  Sporadic and one-dimensional marketing efforts can stifle and prevent your growth.

  Effective marketing requires consistency and a multi-channel approach that meets your perfect customer where they are, whether that's on social media, through email, in person or through direct outreach.

Four

What it Means to Sell Smarter, Not Harder

Four What it Means to Sell Smarter, Not Harder

Selling smarter is about using your resources - time, energy, and money - in the most efficient way possible.

It's about optimising your efforts so every move you make pushes your business forward in a meaningful way that gets you to your goal.

Contrary to what many of us were brought up believing, working harder doesn't necessarily mean you'll see better results, but overextending yourself is a fast track to burnout.

Believe me when I say that from my own experience, this is true.

During the hardest 2 years of my life, I was working as many hours as I possibly could. I was desperately trying to reach out for something that would work, that would get customers to notice me, and to start making the sales I needed to not only be able to pay my mortgage, but to also start paying off the spiralling amounts of debt I was quickly surrounded by.

What happened was, I became lonely, depressed and guilty about the decision I had made to start my own business.

I was working so many hours, I lost friends because I never had the time to give them.

I had no money, so I had to rely on handouts from friends and family to survive.

It was only when I decided to take the leap, put myself into even more debt and trust in a business coach that

I was able to see the strategies and systems I had been missing.

Only then was I able to finally claim my time back and actually start turning my business into the success it became.

And that is why I'm writing this book for <u>you</u>.

I don't want to misguide you here and say that this process was easy. It wasn't.

I had to un-learn the thoughts and the beliefs I had about myself and the way I thought I should run a business, and that is likely going to be barrier you'll come across too.

You will have been having these conversations in your head, telling yourself to behave in a certain way just because you think you should. You will have had family and friends, who through no fault of their own, and with your best interests at heart, will have been imparting their thoughts and their beliefs on to you.

I want you to go through the pages in this book with an open mind knowing that for you to have your products be seen and sold, you are likely to have to do some things that make you feel a little uncomfortable.

You will learn new strategies and skills, which means unlearning some of the actions you have been using so far.

But here is what I promise you...

Four What it Means to Sell Smarter, Not Harder

> ...I won't ask you to do anything I haven't tried myself
>
> ...I will do all that I can to ensure that you never feel the way I felt all those years ago.

When I talk about selling smarter, it means:

- Using strategies backed by data to understand what works, what doesn't and most importantly, why.

- Building genuine customer relationships based on trust and delivering exceptional value, rather than just pushing for the next sale.

- Automating repetitive tasks and delegating jobs to others so you can focus on strategic growth, not the day-to-day grind.

By focusing on what truly matters and removing the inefficiencies that are currently holding you back, you will start to see your business grow without working yourself to exhaustion.

In the following chapters, we'll explore how to navigate these challenges and implement strategies that will help you to sell smarter, so you can focus on what you love most - creating, innovating, and connecting with the people who believe in you and your products.

Four What it Means to Sell Smarter, Not Harder

Nothing is mysterious about finding more customers that want and need your products.

You are only a few small shifts away from creating marketing campaigns that will get your products seen and sold.

Your business will go from an expensive hobby to being able to support your life and that of your family too.

Five

The 4 Pillars of a Wildly Successful Product Business

Five The 4 Pillars of a Wildly Successful Product Business

There are just 4 key things every product business owner needs to focus on to become wildly successful:

Connect | **Nurture** | **Sales** | **Mindset**

When you streamline your focus on these pillars each and every day, you'll see your results skyrocket faster than you ever imagined. These four areas form the foundation of any successful business, and the truth is, if you're not consciously working on them, you're probably stuck in what I call "faux action".

Running around, working hard, being busy every day but not on the right things. So you have little to show for it at the end of each month.

Let's break these 4 essential pillars down, so you can fit them into your daily life and focus on the areas that actually help you to attract more of the right customers, make more sales and feel more confident about your product business.

Pillar 1: Connect

This is where it all begins. Connecting with your perfect customers is the lifeblood of your business.

After all, without customers, you don't have a business. You just have a product that sits there gathering dust.

So, the first step in creating a wildly successful business is figuring out who your perfect customer is and how to get in front of them.

Throughout this book, we'll dive deeper into how to identify and understand your perfect customer. But for now, remember this: **connecting is about building relationships.**

It's not enough to throw a bunch of ads or social posts out into the world and hope for the best. You need to meet your customers where they are - on the platforms they use, with the messaging that resonates with their needs, and with the authenticity that builds trust.

Think about the brands you love. You're likely loyal to them because they connect with you in a meaningful way, not because they scream for your attention.

Example: *Let's say you run a natural skincare brand. Instead of running generic ads, you should be focusing on connecting with people who are already looking for solutions you provide - maybe it's people struggling with acne, or those interested in natural skincare. You create content or run ads that address their specific concerns and show how your product fits into their lives. You show them the transformation your product can achieve and the way others have felt after using it.*

That's connection.

Focus on connecting every single day, whether it be online or in-person. Post on social media, engage with comments, attend events, hold workshops, master classes, or work with other small businesses.

Do it consistently and watch your customer base grow.

Pillar 2: Nurture

Once you've made that initial connection with your customers, your next focus should be nurturing those relationships. Yes, It's great to get a customer to make their first purchase, but that's not enough to build a wildly successful business.

You need them to come back again and again.

One-hit wonders won't sustain your business.

Think about this: the cost of gaining a new customer is much higher than keeping an existing one, so why not spend time nurturing your relationships?

You need to build loyalty, trust, and engagement with your customers so they keep choosing you over somebody else. This means creating touch-points that remind them of your value and give them a reason to return.

You can do this with email marketing, social media engagement, personalised promotions, loyalty programs, or even a well-timed thank-you note.

Example: *If you sell home-made candles, don't let the relationship end after that first sale. Send follow-up emails offering tips on how to get the most from their candle, remind them when new scents are released, or give them an exclusive reason to return sooner. The goal is to stay front of mind and give them reasons to keep coming back.*

Nurturing your customers should be a daily task.

Automate your post purchase thank-you email sequence, set up a loyalty program, respond to DMs, create polls to gather feedback, create a VIP list, share helpful tips and tutorials, surprise and delight customers in their orders. These small actions will create long-term customers that see the value you provide and how much you genuinely care.

Pillar 3: Sales

Next comes sales, which is all about maximising the value of every single purchase. **You don't just want customers; you want customers who come back more often and spend more each time they do.**

There are several smart ways to do this:

- Upgrades
  Offer customers an option to upgrade to a premium version of the product.

- Cross-selling
  Suggest complementary products that enhance the experience of their main purchase that can give them a bigger, better or faster result.

- Bundles
  Offer product bundles that increase the perceived value and encourage customers to buy more.

- Free shipping thresholds
  Encourage customers to add more to their cart to qualify for free shipping.

This is where many businesses often leave so much money on the table.

They focus on just getting sales, but not increasing the average order value (AOV). The trick here is to create <u>IRRESISTIBLE OFFERS</u> that make sense for your customer and enhance their experience with your brand (I'll show you exactly how to create your irresistible offer later on in this book).

Example: *If you're selling fitness equipment, you can offer a workout guide that complements the equipment or bundle related products like resistance bands and water bottles. It's not just about getting one sale; it's about making sure the customer leaves with everything they need - and then some.*

Working on your sales strategy should be a daily activity. Look for ways to increase AOV by fine-tuning your offers, testing bundles, and tracking your results.

Pillar 4: Mindset

Lastly, we have mindset, which may be the most important pillar of all.

Without the right mindset, you won't have the confidence or belief to push through the inevitable challenges of running a successful business.

Mindset is all about coming back to your "why," believing in your ability, and staying consistent even when things get tough.

Building a business is hard work, but the right mindset can

make all the difference between success and failure. If you're constantly doubting yourself or if you're afraid of taking risks, your business will stagnate.

You have already taken the biggest risk of all by starting your business, so now you need to keep pushing forward and always keep the reason why you started in the front of your mind to help you keep going.

It's important to believe in the value of your product, the impact you can have, and your ability to succeed.

Example: *Let's say you've launched a new product, but it isn't performing as well as you expected. Instead of panicking and retreating, a growth mindset would encourage you to analyse what went wrong, learn from it, and improve. Maybe your messaging was off, or maybe your audience wasn't the right fit. Either way, it's a learning experience, and your mindset will determine how you move forward.*

Work on your mindset daily. Surround yourself with positive influences, set realistic goals, and constantly remind yourself why you started this business in the first place. Confidence, resilience, and determination will propel your business forward.

Why Focus on All 4 Pillars Every Day?
The key to success isn't about focusing on one thing and neglecting the rest.

It's about creating a balanced strategy that incorporates all four pillars: Connect, Nurture, Sales, and Mindset. When you give each of these pillars attention every day, you'll see exponential growth. Your customers will feel connected to your brand, they'll keep coming back for more, and your sales will increase - all while you maintain the mindset of a true leader.

So, ask yourself: Where are you spending most of your time right now? If you're focusing on just one or two of these areas, you're likely stuck in faux action - busy but not productive.

But when you streamline your focus and dedicate daily action to all four pillars, your business will transform.

Action Step:
How to Incorporate the 4 Pillars Into Your Daily Life

Now you understand the importance of focusing on Connect, Nurture, Sales, and Mindset every day, it's time to create a plan.

Use the following exercise to assess where you are currently spending your time and identify how you can start incorporating each of these pillars into your daily routine...

Step 1: Self-Assessment

Take a few minutes to honestly evaluate how much time you're spending on each pillar right now.

Connect:
How often are you actively working on reaching and connecting with new potential customers?

Rarely   Occasionally   Regularly

Nurture:
How consistently are you nurturing relationships with existing customers and encouraging repeat purchases?

Rarely   Occasionally   Regularly

Sales:
How often are you working on increasing your average order value through strategies like cross-selling, upgrades, and bundles?

Rarely   Occasionally   Regularly

Mindset:
How much time do you dedicate to your mindset? This could be self-reflection, goal setting, or strengthening your confidence and resilience?

Rarely   Occasionally   Regularly

Step 2: Set Daily Habits for Each Pillar

Now that you've assessed where you are, it's time to create simple daily habits to ensure you're giving attention to all four pillars.

For each pillar, list one small action you can take every day. Keep it realistic!

Connect:
What can you do to reach new customers today?

> Example: I will post one piece of valuable content on social media or reach out to a potential customer

My Daily Action:
_____
_____
_____

Nurture:
How can you strengthen relationships with existing customers today?

> Example: I will send a follow-up email or a thank-you note to a recent customer

My Daily Action:
_____
_____
_____

Five *The 4 Pillars of a Wildly Successful Product Business*

Sales:
How can you increase the value of every sale today?

> **Example:** *I will test a product bundle offer or add an up-sell option on my website*

My Daily Action: _____

_____

_____

Mindset:
How will you work on your mindset today?

> **Example:** *I will spend 10 minutes reviewing goals and affirming my belief in my business*

My Daily Action: _____

_____

_____

Six

What is Mindset Marketing?

Six What is Mindset Marketing?

When I say the word 'Mindset' what springs to mind?

After reading the last chapter you'll probably answer something to do with beliefs and positive thoughts, and that's what many of my clients say back to me as well.

But, there is such a thing as using mindset in your marketing too.

It's the way you CONNECT with your perfect customer on the deepest level in your messaging. It's understanding their fears, frustrations, irritations, and problems, as well as their wants, needs, goals and desires.

This is how you activate the part of your customer's brain that allows them to feel seen and understood, which means they are more likely to trust you quickly and go on to make a purchase.

This includes **actually** understanding why your perfect customer is looking for your product.

You should know the answers to the following questions:

- What's going on in their life that is making them look for what you sell?

- What are they typing into their search engine in the hopes your product will appear?

- How will your product help solve a problem for them?

- How will your product help to make them feel more desirable?

Many people don't realise that 95% of our customers' buying rationale happens subconsciously.

This means your customers are making their purchases based on their emotions.

Sometimes these are called 'gut feelings' or 'impulse buys', however, they are the very opposite of being a spontaneous whim, these decisions come down to their emotions and subconscious feelings.

Here's why it matters

When you can CONNECT and impact your perfect customer on their subconscious level, it can be an absolute game changer for your business!

Emotions and subconscious behaviours overwhelmingly influence customer buying patterns, no matter what you are selling or where you are selling from.

When I realised this, I was able to take my small business to the next level. I have helped multiple other small businesses reach new customers, gain their trust, and make more sales as a result.

These strategies have changed my entire business and my life. And now, I'd like to share a few of them with you, so that you can dramatically improve YOUR business and your life too.

Six What is Mindset Marketing?

Over the last 20 years, here's what I've discovered:

> *You won't make any more sales, any more money or any more profits by just reading books, going through coaches' social media feeds or listening to podcasts alone.*
>
> *You need to take ACTION.*

Read that again...

Selling is about having the right mindset, the right skill set and proven marketing strategies, along with the right actions that work together.

Without these you will keep juggling all of the balls, spinning all of the plates, waking up in cold sweats, and stuck in a rut for months or even years to come.

Six *What is Mindset Marketing?*

Get expert support to start and grow your Product Business

Book your free discovery call today

Seven

Finding Your Perfect Customers

(Hundreds or even thousands of them)

Seven Finding Your Perfect Customers

So, now I've explained what mindset marketing is, the question becomes...

How do you use it to:

- Stand out in a crowded market.
- Create an advantage over your competitors.
- Get your perfect customers hooked on your products.
- Create an unstoppable business that gives you the life style you deserve.

First, we need to create your 'Perfect Customer Profile'.

As we all know, without customers who need or want your product, you have no business.

Even if you offer something that can significantly benefit your customers, if they aren't convinced they need it or that it will help them, they won't be buying.

To create the demand that you need, you MUST work out the person who is most likely to buy your product (and come back again and again).

When you do this, you can start to create content and marketing that speaks directly to them and the way they feel.

What is a perfect customer profile?

Seven Finding Your Perfect Customers

In a very simplified manner, the perfect customer profile contains their age, interests, hobbies, and preferences.

This awareness and understanding helps you to make decisions when building any marketing campaign, your website or your social media posts so you can effectively stand out in front of them.

By the end of this chapter, you'll know:

- Where your perfect customer is spending most of their time.

- What platform your perfect customer uses the most.

- What tone of voice will resonate with your perfect customer the most.

- What images will connect with your perfect customer the most.

Example: *let's say you are a food and drink vendor about to open a cafe / bar in a built up residential area and you want to start a marketing campaign spending little money to bring in more traffic and drive awareness.*

Having put together your perfect customer profile, you know they are local professional workers, it doesn't matter what gender they are, they're between the ages of 30-40, are likely to work from home, they start their day with a cup of coffee, have spare time in the evening and have money to spend on themselves.

Seven Finding Your Perfect Customers

What type of marketing do you think would most help this business stand out to their perfect customer?

- A Linkedin outreach campaign where they reach out to locals and let them know about their new venue?

- Flyers to the residents in the surrounding area with an irresistible offer?

- A pop up in the local area showcasing what they are going to offer and giving each person a reason to come back & buy again?

If you answered 2 or 3 you would be correct!

- Linkedin might be useful for other things, yet perhaps not for bringing in new customers. Their perfect customer is probably not on the look out for new cafe or bar while on that platform.

- Sending flyers out to all the local residents would, however, create a massive amount of brand awareness, and share with future customers the business story and what's available, while including an irresistible offer to come and try it out.

- A pop-up in the local area before the shop is open would also help to showcase the types of things on offer, help the owner get to know the locals and give customers a further reason to come back again.

What makes a great customer profile?

A great customer profile is built in 9 sections, and each of these sections is just as important as the others.

Seven *Finding Your Perfect Customers*

So let's go through and build your perfect customer profile together... no skipping ahead!

I promise that although this might take some time for you to go through and fill out properly, the answers you write down here will pay off for years to come so it is well worth putting in some time and getting it right now.

Seven Finding Your Perfect Customers

Section 1 - An Identity

We'll start off gently by giving your perfect customer a specific name. This is the first step to creating a persona that you can visualise and refer to whenever you do anything for your business, from marketing to the layout of your products or your website.

You should be thinking, "What would X think about this?" for every business decision you make.

You may be starting to realise that you need to build a strong relationship with your perfect customer

TIP - *Who is one of your current perfect customers? You can pick their name if you like!*

> **Exercise:**
>
> What will your perfect customer's name be?

Seven Finding Your Perfect Customers

Section 2 - Motivation

TIP - Think about what's going through your perfect customers mind as they are searching and why they will be looking for your product specifically.

> **Exercise:**
>
> What are the wants, needs or desires for the type of person searching for your product?

Section 3 - Pain Points

Lots of customers are driven to make purchases because they want to solve a problem, frustration, irritation or fear. Understanding these feelings will help you to create messaging, write product descriptions and improve your product to solve these problems in the best possible way.

TIP - *If you struggle to see the problems or frustrations your perfect customer might be facing, consider their daily life and the people around them.*

Exercise

What problems or frustrations is your perfect customer facing?

Are these daily, weekly or other?

Would they consider these to be big or small?

How will your product solve these problems to make their lives better, easier or more fulfilled?

Seven Finding Your Perfect Customers

Here's a table of the most common products people say they can't find problems or frustrations for and some answers that get them going:

Problem / Frustration

Alcohol	Sweets	Underwear	Jewellery	Homeware
Pairing with Food	Health and Diet Restrictions	Comfort	Skin Sensitivities	Durability
Social Pressure to drink	Guilt and Indulgence	Fit and Size Inconsistency	Price vs. Value	Sustainability
Hangovers and Side Effects	Allergies and Sensitivities	Breathability and Fabric	Ethical Sourcing	Easy Maintenance
Quality vs. Cost	Taste vs. Quality	Appearance and Style	Sizing and Fit	Delivery and Assembly
Flavour Complexity	Ethical Sourcing	Specific Needs	Maintenance and Care	Customisation
Social Judgment on Price	Gifting and Presentation	Functionality for Different Activities	Security and Safety	Comfort
Taste Preferences	Animal Free	Invisibility Under Clothing	Emotional Significance	Quality

Section 4 - Influencers

You want your **perfect customer profile** to have a 360° view of your perfect customer. This means including information about their personal and professional lives.

When you include information about their hobbies, likes, dislikes, and where they work from, you can create a whole picture that gives you a huge amount of clarity when it comes to marketing your business and being able to stand out.

TIP - *If you're unsure, ask your current perfect customers, send out a questionnaire or run polls on social media.*

Exercise:

What does your perfect customer do for work?

Where do they work from?

What do they do for hobbies or fun?

Where do they do these things?

How do they prefer to socialise?

Section 5 - Demographics
The easiest way to understand the demographics of your perfect customer is to look at your current average buyer.

TIP - *If you are brand new and haven't started selling yet write down your preferred perfect customer demographics instead.*

Exercise:

Where do they live?

What type of neighbourhood do they live in?

What age are they? (be as specific as possible)

What gender are they? (not always essential)

What is their average income?

Section 6 - A Purpose

By understanding you perfect customers wants and needs, you can discover whether you need to convince them that they need your product, or are they actively searching for your solution.

TIP - *If you are unsure ask your current customers, run polls, adverts, host Q&As, go to the spaces they spend time and ask them.*

Exercise:

Does your perfect customer know they have the problem your product solves?

Is the problem big enough that they are actively looking for a solution?

How does your product communicate it is the best thing for them?

Do you need to convince your customers that they need to buy **your** product?

Section 7 - A Visual

Having a name is one part of your perfect customer profile but giving them an entire sense of being so that you can actually visualise them helps to solidify your understanding and perception of them.

TIP - I suggest having this image on your desk, on your screen saver and on your phone, in fact put it everywhere you make decisions for your business and carry this image around in your pocket. You should never make any decisions for your business that this person would disagree with.

Exercise:

Choose an image online that fully represents your perfect customer.

Section 8 - Online Activity
Now you need to get deeper and understand where your perfect customer likes to spend their time online, what social media sites they like to use, and how they like to be communicated with.

TIP - *If you are unsure, ask! You will see these tips have a common theme: you shouldn't just guess, source the information from your perfect customers.*

Exercise:

How do they like to communicate? Phone, Email, DM, Messaging app?

What social media platforms do they use?

What websites do they like to visit?

Are they tech savvy?

Section 9 - Buying History

This is where you need to understand whether your perfect customer is already buying products similar to the ones you sell. If so, whether they are regular buyers or one-hit wonders.

Exercise:

Do they have any brands they are loyal to?

If yes, what makes them loyal?

What are their buying motivations? Free samples, trials, discounts, other?

What can you offer that would sway them to start buying from you?

Seven Finding Your Perfect Customers

Well, you made it this far! Give yourself a HIGH FIVE!

By this point you should now have a fairly good understanding of your perfect customer.

Step one, done.

Now, we need to move on to how you use this perfect customer profile you have just created.

I have included below a list of ways that you can use it...

- You can now effectively choose the best platform for your marketing - it's where your perfect customer spends their time.

- You can now effectively create the right tone, look and feel of your marketing (and how it's going to connect on the deepest level with your perfect customer).

- You can now effectively focus your marketing on new, returning or renewing customers with great results.

- You can now effectively come up with irresistible offers for your products that hook your perfect customer in.

- You can now effectively create an emotional response marketing campaign that will attract your perfect customer and generate a HUGE flood of sales and income.

I told you it would be worth the time you took, didn't I?

Seven *Finding Your Perfect Customers*

With all this knowledge I think we are ready to get started!

Now you know who you are marketing your products to, it's time to create the messaging that is going to resonate most strongly with them and turn them from a 'maybe' to a 'YES!'

You see, you need to make sure that you reach your perfect customer with enough **impact** that they will open the Email, pick up their phone, walk into your shop, come to your market stall, or go to your website and start getting into the world your business has created especially for them.

Get expert support to start and grow your Product Business

Book your free discovery call today

Eight

The Mindset Marketing Formula

Step 1 - Attract
↳ **Step 2 - Connect**
  ↳ **Step 3 - Educate**
    ↳ **Step 4 - Action**

The best part about this formula is that you can use it for everything, from social media posts, social media adverts, YouTube, flyers, market stalls, in-store, your website homepage, coupons... literally anywhere!

Step 1 - Attract

Before you can do anything else, your message must first attract your customer's attention. You'll probably do this with an attention-grabbing headline.

The headline you put on any marketing message is the most important part and should be the part you spend most of your time perfecting.

After all, if your perfect customer doesn't read your headline, then they aren't reading anything else you have to say, no matter how well it's written!

If your headline doesn't do its job properly, the rest of your marketing isn't worth the time, effort, and energy you have put into it. No matter what you're doing or where you are trying to attract your customers from, EVERY piece of marketing starts with a headline...

Eight *The Mindset Marketing Formula*

- Your market stall should have a headline that is bigger than your logo telling your potential customers what to expect from your stall.

- Your flyers should have a headline that tells your recipient what to expect from reading your flyer.

- Your brick & mortar store should have posters and an A board with headlines that clearly describe what you're promoting.

- Your website homepage should have a headline to welcome customers and let them know they have landed in the right place for what you provide.

No matter where you're putting it, your headline MUST attract your perfect customers' attention.

The right headline also doubles up as something SO many small business owners don't think about, it immediately qualifies your perfect customer and disqualifies those who aren't going to buy.

A great headline will attract the attention of your perfect customers who genuinely want, need, or desire your product.

These will be your best customers, with the most potential and the biggest lifetime value, which is what makes them PERFECT!

All of those are <u>essential</u> for any successful business.

For your marketing and social media pieces to be effective, you must understand your perfect customers' biggest problems, pains, frustrations, irritations, wants, needs & desires.

This pre-marketing work with the perfect customer persona we have just created, is worth its weight in gold and gives you the material you need to create headlines that really work.

Example: Let's say you own a clothing brand that specialises in luxury activewear for men & women who are style-conscious but lead an active lifestyle and want to be comfortable.

And, let's say you have discovered that your competitors sell their products online using social media to get in front of their potential customers.

You've also learned an important factor to your perfect customer is the way their clothes feel so they can understand the quality and how it fits their body...

BOOM!

This helps you to decide that instead of just being another online store, to host exclusive pop-up shops in busy areas or at events that attract your perfect customer, like fitness expos or gyms. These pop-ups offer more than just shopping - think live styling sessions, personalised fittings and answers to customers burning questions.

You then decide to partner with local or emerging designers to create limited-edition pieces available in certain cities or through special events. This not only adds exclusivity but also taps into the local pride, culture, making the brand feel more connected and bespoke.

You could also use the HOT buttons of your perfect customers alongside your idea to create an attention grabbing headline:

> *"Frustrated with activewear that doesn't fit properly, or feel luxurious?*
>
> *Discover why our approach delivers the perfect experience every time!"*

Right away you are attracting attention, hitting on a key pain point and separating yourself from the competition (giving you the advantage).

Your headline should be the largest font size in your entire piece so that your reader's eye knows exactly which words to read first - and yes, bigger than your logo.

Now it's your turn!

(exercise on the next page)

Eight The Mindset Marketing Formula

Using the information gained about your perfect customer and the knowledge you have about your business, it's your turn to create an attention grabbing headline that highlights the unique value of your product or your business as a whole.

TIP - *Start with a question or statement that resonates with your perfect customer's pain points. Follow with a clear benefit or solution your product offers. Use powerful language that creates urgency or excitement.*

Exercise:

Identify your perfect customer's pain points and desires. Go back to your perfect customer profile to identify the main problems, frustrations, or desires your perfect customer has. Consider how your product specifically addresses these issues.

Define your unique value proposition. Write down what makes your product unique and why it's the best solution for your customer's needs. This could be anything from amazing quality, unique features, or a brand new approach.

Draft Your Headline. Using these insights, draft a headline that directly addresses your customer's pain points and highlights your unique value. Remember your headline should be bold, attention-grabbing, and clearly get across the key benefit or solution your product provides.

Refine

Review your headline to ensure it is clear, engaging, and aligned with your customer's needs. Test it with some of your perfect customers or get feedback from friends, family, or a mentor.

Make changes based on their responses to ensure you get maximum impact.

Refinement Questions:

- Does the headline grab attention immediately?

- Is the headline easy to understand and free of jargon?

- Does it effectively communicate the main benefit or solution your product / business has?

Step 2 – Connect

So, you've attracted the attention of your perfect customer with your headline. Great!

Now you have 1-3 seconds before they move on to something else.

Literally.

You have 1-3 seconds to make a HUGE first impression.

That is why you must go through this process over and over again to keep refining it and make sure it's right and connects in the way it needs to, so that your perfect customer will resonate with it.

Remember your perfect customer is in a world of overload, and you need to be seen, liked and trusted.

Simply getting your customer's attention is not enough to get your message across and make a sale, because only a moment after they've noticed you, you've lost them again... unless you're following a proven cut-through-the-noise marketing formula like this one!

Once you've attracted your customer's attention, you must make sure the very next thing they read holds their attention and that is where the **sub-headline** comes in...

Think of it like this:

- The headline is like standing up at a dinner party and tapping your glass with a spoon to get everyone's attention so you can give a toast.

- The sub-headline is the first line you speak when you actually start giving the toast.

They should be a part of the same conversation, giving your customer more detail after you have grabbed their attention.

You must have heard of an 'elevator pitch' before, right?

It's called that because people were given the time a lift (or an elevator) would reach its floor to get their point across and sell someone on what they were trying to pitch.

Well, that is exactly what you are doing for your perfect customers.

Your sub-headline needs to engage their attention by persuasively promising to provide them with essential information that will resolve one of their biggest problems or help them to achieve their desires.

Your sub-headline will be the second largest font size in your marketing piece and it will be placed directly below or after your headline (still bigger than your logo).

> Leave no room for "what's, if's or maybe's" Your reader's eye must know exactly where to go.

It's your job to guide your perfect customer to what you want them to see and do.

You are in control.

Example: Going back to my example of the activewear company whose headline was...

> **"Frustrated with activewear that doesn't fit properly or feel luxurious?**
>
> **Discover why our approach delivers the perfect experience every time!"**

This company should include a sub-headline that continues their marketing message and incites more intrigue to expand the conversation, so it could say something like...

> **That's why we bring our clothes to you**

They have now told their future perfect customer in a matter of seconds:

- They provide activewear.
- They care about the way their clothes fit their customers.
- They provide luxury.
- They care about the way their customers feel in their clothes.

Eight *The Mindset Marketing Formula*

- They allow their customers to see, feel and wear the clothes before buying.

- They make it convenient for their customer to purchase.

Not bad work for 1-3 seconds eh?

Now it's your turn!

(exercise on the next page)

Eight The Mindset Marketing Formula

Assuming you have gone through each step to create your captivating headline, we are going to go through the following steps to make sure that your brand new headline has an engaging sub-headline that keeps your future customers attention on what you have to say.

TIP - *Continue the conversation started by the headline. Provide more specific information about how you deliver on the promise. Highlight a key feature or benefit that addresses your customer's needs or desires.*

Exercise:

Identify the Key Benefit or Unique Selling Point of your business or product. Write down some of the most irresistible aspects of your product or business that addresses your customer's needs or desires. These should be the focus of your sub-headline. Consider what specific solutions or value your product or business offers that will keep your customer engaged.

Draft Your Sub-Headline. Using the benefits or unique selling points written, draft a sub-headline that expands on your headline. It should provide additional details that build on the promise already made and entice your customer to learn more. Aim for clarity and relevance, while maintaining an engaging tone.

Ensure Clarity and Impact

Review your sub-headline to ensure it is clear and engaging. It should maintain your customer's interest and provide a clear understanding of the additional benefits or features of your product.

> **Refinement Questions:**
>
> - Does the sub-headline effectively expand on the headline?
>
> - Is it clear and easy to understand?
>   (Think primary school language)
>
> - Does it provide engaging information that will keep the customer's attention?
>
> - Ensure the sub-headline is the second-largest text on your marketing piece.
>
> - Make sure it is placed directly below or after your headline.

Test your sub-headline with a sample of your perfect customers or get feedback from friends, family, or mentors. Make changes based on their responses to ensure it resonates well and reinforces the message from your headline.

Step 3 - Educate

OK, so now we are getting somewhere!

You've cleared some space for your message and now you want to give your perfect customer some significant, innovative, juicy information or insight about how your product delivers on the promise you have made in your headline and sub-headline.

This is the lengthiest piece of text in your marketing piece: The Body

Now, not every piece of your marketing will have this section.

For instance, your market stall banner will likely only have the headline, sub-headline and a QR code. Your Website homepage will likely only have the headline and sub-headline with some images and a button (however 'The Body' section should still be found on a more relevant page on your website).

Remember your perfect customer lives in a world of overload and you need your products to be seen and sold!

If your marketing were a lawyer, the headline would be your opening statement.

It's up to the body copy to detail your case by presenting all the benefits, the value, and the relevant evidence to the jury (your perfect customer).

Eight *The Mindset Marketing Formula*

Your body copy must convince your perfect customer that you have the best product for them to either help them solve a problem or achieve their desire in the best way possible.

And simply telling them isn't enough.

You must prove it.

In 'The Body' copy please make sure you really emphasise the benefits they want and not just the features of your product. The biggest and most common mistake many product businesses make is to focus on their product's features, and not it's benefits.

An example for the same active wear company could use...

Tired of activewear that falls short on fit, feel, or style? At BrandX, we understand your frustration. Our luxury activewear is crafted not just to meet, but to exceed your expectations in every way.

Here's how:

Unmatched Comfort and Fit - *Our activewear is designed with your comfort in mind. We use premium, high-performance fabrics that feel incredibly soft against your skin and offer unmatched breathability. Our clothes are engineered with precise fit technology to move with you, not against you. Say goodbye to chafing and pinching - our gear hugs your body in all the right ways, ensuring you stay comfortable whether you're hitting the gym or running errands.*

Exclusive Pop-Up Experiences - To truly experience the luxury and perfect fit of our activewear, we're bringing our products directly to you. Join us at our exclusive pop-up shops. Our schedule of upcoming experiences can be found at pageonwebsite.com. Here, you can participate in live styling sessions, receive personalised fittings, and get answers to all your burning questions from our knowledgeable team. This immersive experience ensures you find the perfect pieces tailored to your lifestyle.

Limited-Edition Collections - Discover our latest limited edition collection! We partner with local and emerging designers to offer limited-edition pieces available only through select events or specific cities. These collaborations not only enhance the uniqueness of our collections but also celebrate local culture and pride, making each piece feel bespoke and special.

Our promise - With BrandX, luxury and performance are no longer mutually exclusive, they're perfectly combined. You won't just receive high-quality activewear; you'll receive an unparalleled experience that supports your lifestyle. Visit our pop-up shops or exclusive events to experience the difference for yourself.

Review 1 - This should back up claims on comfort.
Review 2 - This should back up claims on experience.
Review 3 - This should back up claims on high quality.

Call To Action - Shop the latest collection here

Eight *The Mindset Marketing Formula*

Every single time you launch a new campaign, write a new product description or put out a new social media post...

Think benefits over features, benefits over features.

Now this is something that I really wish I had learned sooner; not every customer is looking for the cheapest product or the best deal.

Most people want great value for money, regardless of how much they are actually spending.

Customers will always be willing to pay a higher price if they understand the value of your product and what they are receiving.

Remember this:

> **The price is only an issue when the value is a mystery.**

Read that again.

If you are a product business owner that is struggling with limiting beliefs in pricing your products to reflect the true value you offer, that sentence has the ability to change the trajectory of your business in the best way possible forever.

That's why it's so important 'The Body' copy in your marketing educates your customers about you and your products' greatest value with crystal clear clarity.

Again, this is why all that work you did in the first few steps is SO valuable.

Without your perfect customer profile and a list of their hot buttons, plus your uniqueness, you will never be able to provide the right information in your marketing that will turn browsers into buyers.

When writing 'The Body' copy it is essential to make careful choices.

While this copy is the longest piece of your marketing, it is still a marketing piece, NOT some infomercial, brochure, or catalogue. Resist the temptation to just throw in every bit of information.

Yes, you have successfully attracted and connected with your perfect customer using your headline and sub-headline but everyone else is fighting for it too, so you only have a minute or 2 to educate your future customer, not all day.

You've guessed it, it's your turn again!

(exercise on the next page)

Together we are going to create a detailed and compelling body copy that educates your perfect customer about the benefits and unique value of your product or business that goes beyond just listing features. We are going to deliver value that speaks directly to the person you want buying from you.

TIP - Introduction: *Briefly reintroduce the main promise from your headline and sub-headline.* **Section 1:** *Detail the first key benefit. Explain how it works and why it's valuable.*
Section 2: *Present the second key benefit. Include examples or evidence in the form of testimonials or reviews to support your claims.*
Section 3: *Describe any additional unique selling points. Highlight their importance and relevance.*

> **Exercise:**
>
> **Identify key benefits and unique selling points.** Go back to the benefits and unique features of your product or business that directly address your customer's pain points or desires. List out these benefits clearly, focusing on how they improve the customer's experience or solve their problems.
>
> **Outline your body copy structure.** Next, you need to organise your body copy into sections that each highlight a key benefit or unique selling point. Each section should provide a detailed explanation of how the benefit is delivered and why it matters to your perfect customer.

Write the body copy

Using the outline you have just created, it's time to write your body copy. Focus on emphasising the benefits of your product or business rather than just listing features.

Use persuasive language and provide specific examples or evidence that supports your claims. Go back to my example for BrandX if you need any further guidance.

Review and refine your copy

Read through your body copy to make sure it is clear, engaging, and focused on benefits. Check that it provides valuable information and supports the promises made in your headline and sub-headline.

> ***Refinement Questions:***
>
> - *Does each section clearly put across a key benefit or unique selling point?*
>
> - *Is the copy persuasive and engaging?*
>
> - *Are there specific examples or evidence that support your claims in the form of reviews?*

Ensure 'The Body' copy is easy to read, think primary school language, and visually appealing. Use headings, bullet points, or highlights to break up the text and make key points stand out.

Get expert support to start and grow your Product Business

Book your free discovery call today

Step 4 - Action

You must **always** end any of your marketing messages with a call to action encouraging your customer to see more of what you provide or to take the next natural step. **This is the most important part of the process.**

If you don't have a call to action for your customer to take at the end of this process all of your hard work has been for nothing.

It doesn't matter if you're creating a social media piece, a direct sales letter, a blog, a flyer, or a section on your website, you need to finish with an offer that shows your customer more of what you can provide
- And make it irresistible.

Why?

If you don't, 99% of people will simply walk away.

Your future perfect customer will not take any action unless you ask them to do so right now, and give them a very good reason.

Your offer has one purpose, and one purpose only: To encourage your future perfect customer to take action... that is why it's referred to as a Call To Action!

Your offer should give your future customer a low or no-risk option for taking the next step in your sales process.

- If you sell low-priced products, the next action step might be to buy.

- If you sell a more expensive product, the next action step might be to request more information, try a sample, or buy an introductory package. This will help you to gain their trust and for them to experience your products as well as your customer service.

Going back to our activewear example from before, their offer might be:

"How to Stay Stylish and Comfortable On-the-Go"

This guide could include:

- Top Tips for choosing the right activewear.
- Wardrobe essentials for the active Professional.
- Style inspiration for creating versatile looks from a few key pieces.
- Care tips for maintaining luxury activewear.
- A special offer for those who download the guide.

The great thing about this is you are positioning yourself as an expert, plus when future perfect customers scan a QR code or click your website to get the guide they will be prompted to leave their name and email.

This means if they don't buy immediately, you can then continue to communicate with them, share your value

Eight *The Mindset Marketing Formula*

and show the benefits of your brand and products.

When you keep in touch using this same cut-through-the-noise formula by providing benefits and value instead of sell, sell, sell you will be able to gain their trust.

This means they will be more likely to buy from you when the time is right.

Now we are going to create your Call to Action (CTA) that encourages your perfect customer to take the next step in your sales process.

(exercise on the next page)

This CTA should be irresistible and offer a low or no-risk opportunity for further engagement with your product.

Define the desired action
Decide on the specific action you want your customer or future customer to take after engaging with your marketing message. This action should be aligned with your product's pricing and sales strategy.

Examples of Desired Actions:

- For low-priced products: Direct purchase.

- For mid-range products: Request more information or sign up for a trial.

- For high-priced products: Download a free guide, request a sample, or sign up for an introductory offer.

Draft your offer
Develop an offer that provides clear value and minimises the perceived risk for your future customer. This could be a free resource, a special offer, or an exclusive opportunity.

Examples of Offers:

- A free eBook or guide related to your product or business.

- A discount or promotional code for first-time buyers.

- A no-obligation trial or sample of your product.

- An exclusive invitation to an event, masterclass or workshop.

Write your Call to Action
Create a concise and persuasive CTA that clearly instructs your customer on what to do next. Ensure it highlights the benefits of taking the action and creates a sense of urgency or exclusivity.

Structure of a Great CTA

- **Action verb**
  Use a strong verb to tell your customer what to do: *for example "Download" "Sign Up" "Get"*

- **Benefit**
  Explain what they will gain from taking this action: *for example: "Unlock exclusive tips" "Save 20% on your first order"*

- **Add urgency or incentive**
  Include a time-sensitive offer or exclusive deal to encourage immediate action: *for example "Limited time only" "Exclusive offer for new subscribers"*

Design your CTA placement
Decide where your CTA will appear within your marketing message to ensure it captures your perfect customer's attention.

It should be positioned prominently, and you may use buttons, links, or QR codes depending on your medium.

Placement tips

- **For digital content**
  Use buttons or hyperlinked text.

- **For print materials**
  Include a QR code or clear, bold text with instructions.

- **For social media**
  Use eye-catching images or graphics that include the CTA.

Test and refine your CTA

I like to split test CTAs to see which has the best response. One simple change can make all the difference as to how it lands with your perfect customer and encourage them to take the action you'd like.

If possible, test your CTAs with a small number of your perfect customers or gather feedback to see how well it performs. Check your engagement metrics to understand its effectiveness and make changes as needed.

Testing tips

- Track click-through rates or response rates to gauge effectiveness.

- A/B test different versions of your CTA to see which performs best.

- Adjust wording, placement, or design based on feedback and performance.

The secret to success isn't about chasing sales, money, or profits.

It's about focusing on the value and benefit you deliver to your perfect customers.

When you prioritise creating genuine value, solving problems, sparking joy, and improving lives...

Everything else will follow!

Nine

Your Irresistible Offer

Nine *Your Irresistible Offer*

By now you've successfully captured your customer's attention and made them feel seen and understood with the no-fluff mindset marketing formula.

There is one final, crucial step that can turn interest into action and significantly boost your sales: **making an irresistible offer.**

An irresistible offer isn't just a discount or a promotional gimmick; it's a carefully crafted proposition that provides your customer with immense value while minimising their perceived risk.

It's the final piece of the puzzle that can turn a passive browser into an enthusiastic buyer.

Why your offer matters
An effective irresistible offer should:

- **Enhance perceived value**
  By highlighting the unique benefits and value of your product, you make it more appealing to your perfect customer.

- **Reduce risk**
  Offering a low-risk or no-risk option lowers the barrier to entry and encourages potential customers to take the plunge.

- **Create urgency**
  Adding a time-sensitive element or a special deal can prompt immediate action and prevent potential buyers from delaying their decision.

- **Build trust**
  An irresistible offer can demonstrate confidence in your product and reassure customers about their purchase decision.

Without a strong offer, you might get your product seen but it isn't likely to be sold.

Now is the time for you to provide a compelling reason for your future customer to act now, otherwise you risk losing their interest and potential sales.

By the end of this chapter, you will have everything you need to make your offer so irresistible your perfect customer will feel sorry if they said no.

In fact, there is one very simple thing you can do that will make you more sales in the next 12 months than you have done in the previous 12 months, and it's the one thing all of the guru's and coaches are keeping from you.

The answer is simple: Put more irresistible offers in front of your perfect customers.

It's that simple, but it's got to be a GREAT offer.

This is why creating your offer in an irresistible way is the most important thing you can do. This is a science. There are steps, ingredients and a process that leads to amazing results.

I'm going to give you the 7 ingredients so you can create the perfect irresistible offer.

Nine *Your Irresistible Offer*

But first, I'm going to share the biggest mistake I see happen time and time again from businesses big and small.

They get to their offer, and they simply use it to try and justify the price.

They say, "it's X amount" and then go on to try and convince you why it's worth that amount of money.

Well, that's **not** a great offer.

You're going to see why over the next few pages.

So, what is an offer?

Well, in the simplest form It's the, I'll give you this in exchange for that. The offer should be so good none of your perfect customers will want to say no.

Your offer should speak to the transformation your customer is going to receive, what your product is going to do for them, and how they're going to feel once they have bought it.

Look at the word, 'Offer'. It's a verb, to offer something, which means it is an act.

Doing it requires action.

But are you offering it in the right way?

All irresistible offers solve a problem.

Nine Your Irresistible Offer

They speak to the desired solution for transforming your perfect customers' life. This means there is a direct correlation with your ability to describe the change that your perfect customer already wants, needs, or desires.

So if you're not speaking to these things, and instead only talking about your business or products features, then you are leaving the potential for your products to be sold at a huge risk.

When you realise this, you're going to understand that this process is the most valuable skill you can learn; this process is the art of selling (in a non-pushy, sale-sy way).

When you can master the ability to take your product and wrap it into an irresistible offer, the sky really is the limit.

It might take some time and it's going to take some work, but it's also going to be worth it.

Let's get in to creating your irresistible offer!

Nine *Your Irresistible Offer*

There are three simple steps that can get you on the road to your amazing, irresistible offer, and they are:

- 1 Here's what I've got
- 2 Here's what it'll do for you
- 3 Here's how to get it

Ta-dah! That simple. Isn't it?

Well, yes, it is.

Like I said before, your offer is the 'this' for 'that'.

Here is an example to make this clearer:

Let's make up an imaginary business that sells premium skincare products. It's been around for years gathering a loyal following.

Now, let's say you've developed a new collection that uses ground-breaking, all-natural ingredients designed to provide deep nourishment and visible results within weeks.

You're ready to offer something exclusive for your loyal customers, who have been with you from the beginning of your business journey.

Here's how you might present your irresistible offer in an email...

Nine Your Irresistible Offer

Subject: The Secret To Radiant Skin

Your Glow Up Starts Now, At Half The Price!

Dear [Customer First Name]
You've trusted us with your skin, now it's time for us to give back in a way we never have before.

Our **BRAND NEW** luxury skincare regime is set to launch at £300 and we think you'll agree that it is worth every penny.

- Boosts healthy radiance

- Refines texture

- Improves fine lines

Each product is infused with organic, sustainably sourced ingredients, expertly formulated to deliver visible results in just two weeks!

For the first time ever, we are offering this collection to you for just £150. That's 50% off!

SHOP NOW

This exclusive set includes:

- **Cleanser:** a refreshing start to your routine, deeply purifying while locking in moisture.

- **Serum:** supercharged with antioxidants, to rejuvenate and firm your skin.

- **Moisturiser:** silky hydration that leaves your skin glowing all day long.

- **Eye Cream:** the secret weapon against fine lines, puffyness, and dark circles.

Nine Your Irresistible Offer

This collection will be launching at full price soon, but you get to unlock it early at half the investment.

We've **never offered a discount on a new collection before**, and once this limited time deal ends, it is gone.

- 88% agreed skin texture looks refined*
- 92% agreed skin looked rejuvenated*
- 97% agreed skin looked healthier*
- 83% agreed skin looked more radiant*

SHOP NOW

Why you need to act fast.

- **Exclusive Access:** you are part of a VIP hand picked group receiving this offer.

- **Save £150:** that's a whole lot of glow for half the investment.

- **Real results:** join thousands who trust our products for visible, radiant transformations.

You're skin deserves this. YOU deserve this.

SHOP NOW

But hurry! This offer must end in 7 days. Once it's gone the collection returns to £300.

Thank you for being part of our journey,
With love,
[Owner Name, Brand Name, Contact Details]

*results based on consumer perception in a two week test on 30 participants.

Here's what just happened

Notice I created something called a price anchor. I anchored the price at £300. I anchored the value because value and price are all relative.

I didn't say: '*I think it's worth that*' or '*I'd like to charge that*', I said: '*This collection is £300*' and it is. This is a statement of fact.

Now, I've already begun to talk about what this collection does and why it's worth every penny. I've included the results our customers get, and how the organic, sustainably sourced ingredients, are expertly formulated to deliver visible results in just two weeks!

I also reinforce the message that our claims have been tried and tested to further build trust and peace of mind that this new range will deliver the results being promised.

The people that receive this offer are already likely to justify the price as well as how to pay for it. In other words, the value of this offer was established quickly and having completed my 'customer profile' I'm able to talk to them as individuals.

They most likely didn't find themselves comparing the price to something cheaper, which is the important thing here, because if you're not careful, your customers are likely to do so.

When they say something like 'it's too expensive', in their mind, they're already comparing what you're selling to something else.

Nine Your Irresistible Offer

What's preventing people buying?

Resistance.

Resistance tends to come out as objections.

A lot of business owners make the mistake of thinking if they don't speak to their customer objections, or if they pretend they don't exist, then they'll go away, but in my experience that just makes it worse.

I want you to follow these 7 steps closely, so you don't end up running the risk of having an offer that isn't irresistible. This would mean you're going to have more objections from your customer and more reasons why not to buy, which will turn in to more no's and more rejection of your products.

Now, it might take you a few tries to make your offer *irresistible*; this isn't the sort of thing that can happen magically, but remember the question I asked at the beginning of this book, **'are you interested, or are you committed?'**

Those who are committed will go through this section and master their irresistible offer. They will be the ones that go on to make more sales than ever before.

Those who are merely interested will gloss over this. They might give it a quick go and think 'I've got this already'... But have they really?

Keep in mind your *why* and go through these steps.

Bookmark this section and keep on refining!

Nine *Your Irresistible Offer*

The 7 ingredients you need to create an irresistible offer

Every single one of these ingredients serves a very specific intention to get your products seen and sold!

They will help you to remove objections, build trust, and encourage your customer to take action.

Let's explore each of them in detail and, most importantly, how you can implement them in your product business.

1 - Promise
The promise is the heart of your offer.

It tells your customer what they can expect when they buy your product, including the specific transformation they will experience. This goes beyond just selling a product, it's about selling the result.

How to create it:

- Start by getting specific about who your product is for. This is your perfect customer, the person who will benefit the most from what you are offering. You should already have this in detail.

- Next, identify the problem they are facing and how your product solves that problem.

- Finally, focus on the transformation. How will your customer feel after they have used your product?

Nine *Your Irresistible Offer*

Example: *if you sell skincare, your promise might be... "Get clear, glowing skin in just 30 days, without harsh chemicals or complicated routines"*

> **Key questions to consider:**
>
> - Who is this product for?
>
> - What problem are they facing?
>
> - What transformation will they experience?

When your promise is clear, it connects with your customer on a deep, emotional level and gives them a reason to care about your product.

2 - Process

The process explains how the transformation happens.

This is your opportunity to give your customers a peek behind the curtain, showing them the step-by-step journey they'll take once they commit to your offer.

How to create it:

- Break down the steps of how your product solves their problem.

- Make it simple and easy to understand, showing them the path from where they are now to where they want to be.

Example: *if you sell gym equipment...*
Include a short video or step-by-step routine showcasing how it can help them achieve their fitness goals in a straightforward way without industry jargon.

Key questions to consider:

- How does this product work?

- What steps will the customer follow to achieve the desired result?

Customers want to feel confident there's a proven method behind your product. Clarifying the process reassures them the transformation you've promised is within reach to them.

3 - Price

Price is more than just a number; it's part of your marketing strategy.

How you price your product says a lot about its value, so it's essential to anchor your pricing in a way that makes your offer feel irresistible.

How to create it:

- Price your product in a way that reflects the value it provides.

- Anchoring the price can be a powerful strategy.

Example: if you sell takeaway coffee...
Pricing a medium coffee at £4.50 and a small at £3.00 anchors customers' perception of value, making the large coffee at £5.00 seem like the obvious choice. This strategy works because the medium price acts as a reference point, and customers see the large as offering significantly more for only a small additional cost.

> **Key question to consider:**
>
> - What is the regular price, and what makes it worth that amount?

Anchoring the price shows your customers they are getting something special at a greater value, helping them feel like they're making a smart investment.

4 - Value Add

This is where you take your offer from good to great.

Adding bonuses or bundling products together increases the perceived value of your offer and makes it harder for your customer to say no.

How to create it:

- Consider what complementary products or services you can include to sweeten the deal.

- Maybe you bundle a product with a free guide, an exclusive masterclass / workshop / event, or a limited-time promotion on their next purchase.

Example: *if you sell kitchen gadgets...*
Add a free recipe book, a personalised cooking guide or a workshop with a local chef for customers who purchase a premium set.

Key questions to consider:

- What can you offer as a bonus that complements the main product?

- How can you increase the overall value of the purchase without significantly increasing costs?

Adding extra value makes your offer feel generous and positions it as a complete solution to your customer's problem.

5 - Risk Reversal

One of the biggest obstacles to purchasing is the fear of making a bad decision. Your customers are asking themselves, "What if this isn't right for me?"

It's your job to eliminate that risk by offering a strong guarantee.

How to create it:

- Consider offering a money-back guarantee or a satisfaction guarantee to reduce the perceived risk.

Example: *"If you don't see results within 30 days, we'll refund your money, no questions asked"*

This shifts the burden of risk away from the customer and onto you, making them feel safe in their decision to buy.

Key questions to consider:

- What fears or doubts might the customer have about purchasing your product?

- How can you alleviate those fears with a guarantee?

A clear, strong guarantee removes the barriers to buying and increases your customer's confidence in making a purchase.

6 - Scarcity & Urgency

Even when customers are interested, they often delay making a purchase.

To prevent this, you need to give them a reason to act now, or they might walk away and never return.

Scarcity and urgency create that reason.

How to create it:

- Create a sense of urgency by limiting the quantity of products available or offering a time-sensitive promotion.

Example: *"Only 20 items left in stock"* or *"This special offer must end at midnight"*

When customers feel like they might miss out, they're more likely to act quickly.

> **Key questions to consider:**
>
> - How can you introduce a sense of urgency to your offer?
> - Can you limit the availability of your product in some way?

Scarcity and urgency push customers to take immediate action, making them feel they will miss out on a great deal if they hesitate.

7 - Storytelling

Storytelling weaves all the above ingredients together.

It is the reason behind why your product exists and why it's the perfect solution for your customer's problem.

Without a compelling story, your offer can feel flat and impersonal.

How to create it:

- Share the story of how your product came to be or how it has transformed the lives of others.

Example: *If you sell handcrafted jewellery...*
Tell the story of how you started designing pieces to celebrate individuality and how each piece is crafted with your customer in mind.

Make the customer feel like they're part of something bigger and show them why you're passionate about what you do.

Remember, your customers will always be asking themselves 'why are you doing something?', 'why have you got a promotion?', 'why are you selling this product this way?'.

It is your job to use storytelling to answer all of these whys. If you leave them unanswered, they will answer them for you. I promise you they won't be as nice about you as you will be.

Key questions to consider:

- What's the story behind your product, and how does it connect with your customer's desires?

- How can you make your customer the hero of the story?

- How can you explain the reasons behind why you are doing what you are doing?

By telling a story that resonates, you give your customer an emotional reason to buy, answering their unspoken question "Why should I buy this?"

Putting it all together

Now that you have the 7 key ingredients, it's time to apply them to your product business.

Whether you're selling handmade goods, tech gadgets, or coffee, every offer you create needs to include these 7 elements.

When combined, they make your offer compelling, clear, and most importantly, ***irresistible***.

Nine Your Irresistible Offer

Here's how to start:

- **1 Define your promise**
  Make sure your promise speaks directly to your perfect customer and clearly outlines the transformation they will experience.

- **2 Clarify your process**
  Show your customer how your product will help them achieve the transformation, step by step.

- **3 Anchor your price**
  Use strategic pricing to make your offer feel like an amazing deal.

- **4 Add value**
  Include bonuses or bundles that increase the overall worth of your offer.

- **5 Reverse the risk**
  Offer guarantees to remove any doubt or hesitation.

- **6 Create urgency**
  Use scarcity or time limits to push customers to act now.

- **7 Tell your story**
  Share the reason behind your product and connect emotionally with your customer.

By mastering these seven ingredients, you'll not only create offers that your customers can't resist, but you'll also build a deeper connection with them, ensuring that your products are seen, loved, and sold.

Nine *Your Irresistible Offer*

offer
/ˈɒfə/

verb
1. present or proffer (something) for (someone) to accept or reject as desired.

Get expert support to start and grow your Product Business

Book your free discovery call today

Ten

Products your Perfect Customer will Love

Ten Products your Perfect Customer will Love

By this point you are now able to use mindset marketing and create an irresistible offer that will get your message seen and understood.

Now we want to ensure the products you are selling are the ones that are going to benefit your perfect customer (and your business) the most.

It's not enough to simply market well, you need to ensure that what you're offering is **exactly** what your audience craves. The right products, designed or curated with your perfect customers in mind, will not only attract them but also keep them coming back for more.

Understand their pain points and desires.

To create products your perfect customer will love, you must first fully understand their pain points, desires, and motivations. It's essential to know not only what problems they're trying to solve but also how they want to feel when they use your product.

I am assuming you know these things already if you have gotten this far, as we walked through this whole process back in chapter 6.

So, please grab your notes and make sure you have gone into as much detail as possible about:

- The daily challenges your perfect customer faces.

- How your product solves these challenges in a way no one else can.

- The emotional response your product creates. (e.g. *relief, joy, pride, confidence*)

Example: *using the fitness apparel brand...*
Their perfect customer may be looking for clothing that's comfortable, luxurious, and stylish, but they might be wanting these products to make them feel confident, empowered, and part of a community of like-minded people. Understanding both their practical needs and their emotional desires allows you to create a product line that speaks to them on multiple levels.

The following action steps will take you through the process of developing or curating products that have the promise to resonate deeply with those who most want them (your perfect customers).

You'll discover how to match your products to your customers' needs and desires, ensuring your product line consistently delivers massive perceived value.

> **Action Step 1 - Survey**
> Take some time to survey your existing customers: go through reviews, feedback and use polls on social media.
>
> - What are their common complaints or unmet needs?
>
> - What features or improvements do they wish your products had?

Use this feedback to refine existing products or develop new products that better serve them.

Action Step 2 - Conduct Market Research
Even with a deep understanding of your customers, you need to stay informed about what's happening in your market. Trends evolve, customer preferences change, and new competitors enter the space which can disrupt the market.

Research:

- Emerging trends that resonate with your perfect customer.

- Gaps in the market where your product could stand out.

- The strengths and weaknesses of your competitors' products.

Staying on top of these changes is crucial for ensuring that your products remain relevant and in demand.

Example: *If you're in the haircare industry...*
You might notice a growing demand for organic, cruelty-free products. By tapping into this trend you can develop new offerings that align with your customers' values, positioning your brand as a leader in that space.

Action Step 3 - Regularly Research your Industry
Set aside time each month to review:

- What your competitors offer.

- Check industry reports.

- Explore what's trending on the social media platforms your customers use.

I also suggest looking through any of your competitors' public reviews to see what they're doing well and what they could be doing better. Please don't be tempted to copy your competitors, this will never make you be seen as the go-to, trusted brand in your niche!

This action step is meant for you to see what your potential customers want more or less of, so you can tap in to what they are currently missing.

Action Step 4 - Start a Waitlist

A great way to see if there is demand for a product you'd like to bring to market is to start a waitlist.

Getting future customers to signal your product idea appeals to them , is a sure-fire hit!

Here's how you can make your waitlist work for you:

- Setup a simple waitlist form on your website to ask any vital questions getting their name and Email address.

- Connect this form to an Email auto-responder so you can then send targeted information to these people. They can then be involved with any further research. To keep them warm, tease the release as you get closer and closer to launch.

- You can use this time to understand how much they already know about your product, what their expectations are when it's released, and the type of price point they might be willing to pay for it.

This is a really simple way for you to get an idea of whether your customers and future customers are thinking the same way as you. This shows that they are interested before committing to a purchase.

The best part of this is when you have a lot of people signing up, it shows there is a lot of interest and proves you have a great idea. Meaning you can then charge a premium for it!

These insights will allow you to tailor your messaging to help you get maximum results.

Example: Glastonbury festival sells out within minutes every single year, yet they don't ever release tickets straight away. You have to first signal your interest and join their waitlist.

They get hundreds of thousands of people to register for the event. Then at a specified date and time the tickets are released. People wait and queue for hours prior to this release in order to try and get one.

Most festivals don't have this approach. They simply put their tickets on sale and actually, many of them don't ever sell out. They never get the same amount of momentum as Glastonbury because of their waitlist strategy.

> **Action Step 5 - Align Products with your Brand Story**
> Your products are a reflection of your brand, so it's important that they align with the story you're telling.
>
> This not only differentiates your offerings but also creates a deeper connection between your products and your customers.
>
> **Think about your brand's values and mission:**
>
> - How can your products embody those values?
>
> - If your brand stands for sustainability, are your products made from eco-friendly materials?
>
> - If your brand is focused on luxury, do your products offer the quality and exclusivity that your customers expect?

Your brand story is a powerful tool for building emotional connections with customers. By ensuring your products align with this story, you can create an experience that reinforces why customers should choose you over anyone else.

Revisit your brand's mission statement and values. Make sure each product in your line-up reflects them.

Example: *if your brand focuses on wellness, do your products promote a healthier lifestyle? Is that message clear in your marketing and product descriptions?*

Action Step 6: Packaging & Presentation Matter
When it comes to selling products, first impressions are **everything**.

Your packaging and presentation should not only be functional, but also reflect the quality and values of your brand.

Review your current packaging & presentation...

- Does it align with your brand's identity?

- Does it create an experience that will delight your customers?

Beautiful, thoughtful packaging can turn a good product into a memorable experience, thereby creating a lasting impression on your customers.

For online businesses, unboxing experiences are a key part of customer satisfaction.

Customers should feel excited and valued when they receive your products.

For brick-and-mortar stores and market stall sellers, eye-catching displays and well-designed packaging can make all the difference in converting browsers into buyers.

If not, consider investing in upgraded packaging or presentation that reflects the value of your products and resonates with your perfect customer.

Action Step 7: Focus on Quality and Consistency
No matter how well you market your products, their long-term success hinges on their quality.

Consistency is equally important:

- Audit your product quality and customer feedback regularly.

- Are there areas where your product can be improved?

- Are customers consistently leaving great feedback, or do you notice recurring complaints?

Customers should know what to expect every time they buy from you. Whether it's the quality of the product itself, the packaging, or the customer service experience, consistency builds trust and loyalty.

High-quality products that consistently deliver on their promises will not only keep customers coming back but also generate word-of-mouth referrals.

Make adjustments where necessary to ensure your products always meet or exceed customer expectations.

Get expert support to start and grow your Product Business

Book your free discovery call today

Eleven

The Customer Growth Journey

Now you have created your perfect product, in this chapter, we're going to break down the four essential products every successful product business needs: the entry level product, the hero product, the product bundle, and the subscription product.

Each one plays a key role in helping you grow your customer base, build trust, nurture customers and increase sales over the long term.

1 - The Hero Product
The Star of Your Business

The hero product is the centrepiece of your entire business. Whether you have 1 of them or you have a few, your hero product is the thing that gets your perfect customers exited, keeps them coming back, and ultimately defines your brand in the marketplace.

The hero product is where you should focus most of your attention because it represents the core offering for your perfect customer and ensures they are getting the best thing that meets their wants, needs, or desires.

Why Focus on One Hero Product?
Focusing on one hero product allows you to tailor your mindset marketing, sales strategy, and customer experience specifically around this product.

By doing so, you create a strong, clear message for your customers that builds trust and builds value.

When customers see you have a product that truly solves a problem or enhances their life in a meaningful way, they are more likely to buy... **and keep buying.**

While it's possible to repeat this process for multiple hero products, I strongly recommend you start with one.

Master this process for one hero product first, and then expand as you gain confidence.

Remember, it is easier to grow and scale 1 product by putting all of your love, attention and focus on to it than it is to grow and scale 10.

By using this process you will be able to put your attention on to your hero product, build trust in the best possible way and encourage customers to buy in to more of what you have as you nurture them.

Action Step: Define Your Hero Product

- What is the product you believe can be the star of your business?

- How does this product solve a problem or fulfil a need for your perfect customer?

- Write down all the reasons your perfect customer would be excited to purchase this product...

2 - The Entry Level Product
Building Trust

Now you have decided on your hero product, we can take a step back and create your entry level product that walks your perfect customer towards your hero product.

An entry-level product is a lower-cost (or free), lower-risk version of what you offer. It's designed to give potential customers a taste of your brand and your value.

This product is crucial because it helps build trust and shows your future perfect customer you are a value up front type of business. When a customer experiences how much value you offer at a lower price point, they are more likely to invest in your higher-priced products, like your hero product.

Why Entry Level Products Matter
The key to getting more people into your world is by giving them something small and manageable that shows off your expertise or product quality.

Think of it as a bridge that helps move someone from being a curious browser to a committed customer.

You can use things like samples, miniature sizes, E-guides, quizzes, workshops or masterclasses as great entry level products that allow your perfect customer to understand more about your business and how you can help them solve a problem or bring them closer to what they desire.

Eleven The Customer Growth Journey

When you create your entry level product you need to consider all of the reasons why your perfect customer **wouldn't** buy your hero product.

In order to create the perfect entry level product you should have answers to these following questions:

- What other similar products has your future customer been using that isn't working for them?

- Why hasn't a similar product given them their desired result?

- How can you prove that your hero product (and your business) is the one for them?

- What extra information should they know about your hero product that isn't immediately obvious?

When you are able to create an entry level product that helps your perfect customer overcome these hurdles or objections you will increase the likelihood of them going on to purchase your hero product.

Action Step: Create Your Entry Level Product

- What can you create or offer at a lower price or free to introduce new customers to your business?

- How does this product complement your hero product?

- List three reasons why this product will make it easier for customers to trust you and walk them towards your hero product being the ultimate thing for them.

3 - The Perfect Product Bundle
Offering More Value

If you are filling this in as we go through, by now you have created your hero product, the thing that you want your business to be known for and you have decided which entry level product will best answer their fears or objections and walk them towards your hero product.

Now we are going to use the following two product types to nurture these customers and keep providing them with value whilst building further trust.

Eleven The Customer Growth Journey

The one we are going to look at first is The Perfect Product Bundle – and I have named it this because this isn't just any product bundle, this is showing your perfect customer just how much you see and understand their needs by making their life even easier!

The best type of product bundle takes your hero product and enhances it by grouping it with other complementary products or services.

This type of bundle is powerful because it increases the perceived value and helps your customers get bigger, better or faster results.

From my experience, three is the magic number when creating the perfect product bundle. It's just enough to offer variety without overwhelming and confusing your customer.

Why Bundles Work...
When you position your hero product as the central piece and surround it with related items, you're showing your customers that you truly understand their needs and their desires.

Whether it's offering accessories or services that support the hero product, a well-thought-out bundle can deliver more value and make the purchase decision even easier for your customers.

The Two Types of Perfect Product Bundle
There are two types of the perfect product bundle, both of these hold your hero product as their centre piece but what's included around them can differ.

Type 1: In this Perfect Product Bundle you should include three products, the first is your hero product and the other two should help your perfect customer achieve their desired result from your hero product in an even bigger, better or faster way.

Consider this when creating this type of bundle, you have successfully introduced a new customer to your business and your hero product – now you want to show that customer just how much you care about them and what else you have on offer.

So don't ever have a 'this will do' attitude. Seriously consider how they want to feel when they buy your hero product and then think about everything else you have on offer that will increase that feeling and show them that you are making their life easier.

Type 2: In this Perfect Product Bundle you should include 2 products and a service – If you don't provide any services keep reading as you don't actually have to which is what makes this brilliant!

This Bundle will once again have your hero product as its centrepiece and include one other product that enhances the results your perfect customer has but now, we want to include a voucher for a service that will extend the life of your hero product.
This is where you are going to foresee any problems, frustrations or irritations that your perfect customer might have with your hero product further down the line and provide a direct resolution for them, showing them the ultimate trust!

Eleven *The Customer Growth Journey*

Example: *if your hero product is a blouse, you could include a complementary accessory with the blouse plus a voucher for a dry cleaners, or for a tailor. Both of these are considering what your perfect customer will be doing with your hero product and providing them with a way to do it while introducing them to a service provided by another small business, now we are networking too!*

Like I said at the start of this, you don't need to provide these services yourself. Find another reputable small business that provides the services your hero product would benefit from the most and provide the help your perfect customer might need further down the line.

Approach them, let them know you would love to include a voucher for their services and introduce your customers to their business, is there a way in which you can work together and for them to either provide you with that voucher to get the customer to notice their business, or can you purchase vouchers from them at a discounted rate.

Now you aren't just showing your perfect customer that your business is the one that knows them best, you are also helping introduce them to other products that you provide in the best way possible, plus you are helping introduce customers to other small businesses who you know they would benefit from too.

This is The Perfect Product Bundle in action!

Action Step: Build Your Perfect Product Bundle

- List all the benefits and the feelings your hero product provides your perfect customer.

- What two products will create The Perfect Product Bundle to enhance these benefits?

- What service would benefit your customer further down the line and show them how much you know and understand their needs?

- Who is reputable that provides this service and how can you work with them?

- Think back to the mindset marketing formula and write down a headline and sub-headline for your Perfect Product Bundle that speaks directly to the thoughts and feelings of your perfect customer.

4 - The Subscription Product
Ensuring Recurring Revenue

The final product every wildly successful product business needs is a subscription product.

This is where you can take your hero product and offer it on a regular basis so customers don't have to think about reordering. This removes any purchase barriers as it can be set up to arrive at regular intervals.

Your subscription product ensures a steady flow of income for your business ensuring you don't start each month from zero and makes it incredibly easy for your perfect customer to keep purchasing from you.

There are two distinct types of subscription products your business can choose from:

Type 1: Hero Product Subscription
Customers receive your hero product at regular intervals without needing to reorder. This keeps them engaged, loyal and has been proven to retain customers within businesses for longer.

Type 2: Curated Subscription Box
Consider the results and feelings your hero product provides, as this is the thing that has attracted your perfect customer to your business in the first place. You can create a subscription box with products that provide complementary results and feelings. Try collaborating with other small businesses to add extra value and surprise your customers with exclusive products each month.

Eleven The Customer Growth Journey

> **Action Step: Develop Your Subscription Product**
>
> - What could your business offer as a subscription?
>
> - How would this subscription make your customers' lives easier?
>
> - Can you partner with other businesses to add unique items to your subscription box?
>   List two businesses you could collaborate with to get you started.

Wrapping Up the Customer Growth Journey

By implementing all four of these essential products: entry level product, hero product, product bundle, and subscription product, you're setting the foundation for long-term success.

You'll attract more perfect customers, build stronger relationships, and ultimately create a business that keeps growing over time.

Eleven The Customer Growth Journey

Get expert support to start and grow your Product Business

Book your free discovery call today

Twelve

S.E.R.V.I.C.E

Twelve S.E.R.V.I.C.E

I mentioned earlier that 'customers expect more than just a product and average customer service. They want, no, they demand an experience. Businesses that fail to deliver consistent, engaging, and personal experiences often struggle with customer retention.'

That is exactly why I wanted to include a section dedicated to my S.E.R.V.I.C.E method.

I speak to so many business owners that claim they give amazing, blow-your-socks-off customer experiences; however, after just a few questions it seems there are very few that actually live up to the hype they create for themselves around this.

Exceptional customer service is no longer a "nice-to-have". It's an absolute necessity if you want your product business to thrive and allow it to provide for you and your family for years to come.

Whether you're selling online, in a physical store, or at a market stall, how you treat your customers can be the difference between a booming business and one that struggles to keep up.

That's why I developed the S.E.R.V.I.C.E Method, a comprehensive approach to elevate your customer service game to world-class levels.

By focusing on these seven core elements, you can build customer loyalty, increase sales, and allow your business to truly stand out...

Twelve S.E.R.V.I.C.E

Standards

Educate

Relate

Value

Inform

Care

Experience

Standards
Setting a High Bar and Sticking to it

Consistency in service is non-negotiable. Customers want to know that they'll receive the same excellent treatment every time they interact with your brand.

Consistency builds trust.

Put yourself in your customers' shoes:

One day, you walk in to a shop and you're greeted warmly by an employee who helps you find the perfect product. You leave after having a great experience and buying the recommended product. You decide to go back a few weeks later to buy something else that caught your eye, and find the service lacklustre. You aren't given the same attention, the same help, or the same enthusiasm.

How would it make you feel?

That the first time was the fluke!

The issue with inconsistency is people automatically assume the positive experience was the one-off and the negative experience is the way you would usually deal with customers.

This can be incredibly damaging, making the customer question the quality of your business and the products you sell.

Twelve S.E.R.V.I.C.E

Action Step:

- **Standardise Your Processes**
Create clear guidelines for handling customer interactions across all platforms. If you have a team, train them regularly to follow these standards rigorously.

If you are on your own, make sure you aren't stressed when responding to customer queries and make sure you have a lunch break during the day if you're dealing with customers face to face.

The difference between having some time to sit and relax throughout your day or not can make a huge impact on how you treat customers.

- **Quality Control**
Regularly ask for customer feedback and monitor interactions to ensure your service remains consistent.

- **Training**
Continuous staff training ensures everyone is aligned with your brand values and service standards.

I highly recommend training staff monthly to reinforce how they should interact with your customers and deal with any questions, queries, or problems.

Twelve S.E.R.V.I.C.E

Educate
Help Your Customers

Education adds value beyond the sales transaction.

When you teach customers how to use or care for your products, you create more meaningful relationships. This shows just how much you care about them and what you're selling.

You're not just selling; you're helping!

This not only improves their experience but also builds trust in your expertise and knowledge.

Action Step:

- **Product Guides and Tutorials**
  Offer e-guides, tutorials, or how-to videos that showcase how to use your products effectively and how to pair them with others.

- **Transparent Policies**
  Make return policies, shipping information, and important details easy to understand and find.

- **Events, Workshops, Masterclasses and Webinars**
  Host live events to educate customers and showcase your expertise. From going live on social media, to hosting a workshop in your store. There are numerous ways you can educate your customers both online and in-person that will deliver value and build trust.

Twelve S.E.R.V.I.C.E

Relate
Building Genuine Connections with your Customers

Customers don't want to be just another number.

People crave to be seen and understood. Especially when we're parting with money for a product or service.

Building genuine relationships will turn first-time buyers into repeat customers and turn repeat customers in to loyal fans!

> *Action Step:*
>
> - **Share Testimonials**
>   Showcase real customer stories to build social proof and make your brand relatable. Share them absolutely everywhere and often.
>
> - **Tell Your Story**
>   Share why you started your business and how your products solve real problems or help customers achieve their desires. A heartfelt story can create emotional connections.
>
> - **Engage Actively**
>   Respond to comments, answer questions, and engage with your audience to show you care.

Twelve S.E.R.V.I.C.E

Value
Offering Something Extra

In a world full of choices, value is what sets you apart.

It's not just about what your product does, it's about what additional benefits or perks your customers get when they choose you.

Action Step:

- **Highlight USPs**
  Emphasise what makes your products or your business unique, whether it's quality, ethical sourcing, or craftsmanship.

- **Exclusive Promotions**
  Offer loyalty programs or limited-time promotions for repeat customers.

- **Added Value**
  Provide extra resources, like free e-books or access to exclusive communities, to offer more than just a product and encourage customers to become a part of your 'world'.

Twelve S.E.R.V.I.C.E

Inform
Clear and Honest Communication

No one likes feeling left in the dark. The more informed your customers feel, the more they'll trust your brand.

This starts with clear, transparent communication.

From the moment they land on your website to post-purchase follow-ups, ensure they're informed at every step of the journey.

Offering transparency helps avoid unnecessary frustration and builds trust.

Action Step:

- **Detailed FAQ Section**
  Have a comprehensive FAQ on your website to answer common customer questions about shipping, returns, and more.

- **Clear Contact Information**
  Make it easy for customers to get in touch through various channels - email, phone, live chat, or social media.

- **Regular Updates**
  Keep customers informed about new products, shipping updates, and policy changes to build transparency and trust.

Twelve S.E.R.V.I.C.E

C are
Supporting your Customers after the Sale

Customer care doesn't end after a purchase. Ensuring that customers feel supported even post-sale can turn one-time buyers into lifelong customers.

How you follow up post-purchase is as important as the sale itself.

It shows you care about their journey, not just their money.

> ### Action Step:
>
> - **Follow-Up Emails**
>   I recommend you follow a 3-4 Email post purchase sequence that thanks customers for their purchase, gives further value, asks for feedback and offers an incentive to buy from you again.
>
> - **Service Check-Ins**
>   If a customer had an issue, follow up to ensure they're happy with the resolution.
>
> - **Surprise and Delight**
>   Surprise your customers with a handwritten thank-you note or a small gift with purchase to leave a lasting impression.

Twelve S.E.R.V.I.C.E

Experience
Creating a Memorable Journey

From the moment a customer lands on your website, walks into your store to the unboxing of your product at home, every touchpoint should enhance the overall experience.

A memorable experience keeps customers coming back for more and telling others about you too.

Action Step:

- **User-Friendly Website**
  Ensure that your website is easy to navigate and mobile-friendly for a seamless shopping experience.

- **In-Store Ambience**
  If you have a physical store / market stall, pay attention to the environment: lighting, music, and scent. Try and engage as many of the senses as possible to create a welcoming atmosphere and to ensure you're remembered!

- **Personalised Service**
  Use customer data to tailor their experience, such as sending personalised recommendations or offering birthday promotions.

Twelve S.E.R.V.I.C.E

Incorporating the S.E.R.V.I.C.E Method into your business can drastically enhance how your customers perceive and interact with your brand.

Positioning your business to stand out in a competitive market, ensuring you become
seen and sold!

Twelve S.E.R.V.I.C.E

Get expert support to start and grow your Product Business

Book your free discovery call today

Thirteen

Making Bold Decisions

Thirteen Making Bold Decisions

Congratulations! You've made it to the final chapter!

You've explored proven strategies to sell smarter, not harder. You've learned how to build trust, create meaningful customer relationships, deliver exceptional service, and position your products for success.

But there's one final ingredient that will determine your ability to implement everything you've learned: **confidence**.

Confidence is what will empower you to take bold steps, make game-changing decisions, and overcome the inevitable challenges that come with running a successful product-based business.

This final chapter is all about building the confidence to take action, because all the knowledge in the world won't get your products seen and sold unless you have the self-belief to make it happen.

Fixed Mindset vs. Growth Mindset
Which Do You Have?

I spoke about Mindset Marketing earlier in this book, which was all about the way you **connect** with your perfect customer on the deepest level by understanding their fears, frustrations, irritations, and problems, as well as their wants, needs, goals and desires.

I now want to look at what Mindset means for you and how you view your business, your challenges, your successes, and your setbacks.

Thirteen *Making Bold Decisions*

You see, it can either be a powerful tool for growth or a significant barrier to your progress. In particular, the difference between a fixed mindset and a growth mindset has the ability to make or break your success.

Fixed Mindset
Stuck in the Comfort Zone

A business owner with a fixed mindset believes their abilities, talents, and intelligence are static. They can't change much, no matter how hard they try. This mindset leads to avoiding challenges, fearing failure, and sticking to what's familiar.

Here are some common traits of a fixed mindset and an example of what they look like in daily practice:

- **Avoids Challenges**
  Prefers to stay within their comfort zone, avoiding new strategies or taking decisions they deem too risky and could lead to failure.

- **Fears Feedback**
  Sees criticism and negative feedback as a personal attack rather than an opportunity to learn and grow their business.

- **Gives Up Easily**
  When faced with obstacles, tends to throw in the towel quickly rather than find alternative solutions that can help them get through.

- **Plays It Safe**
  Sticks to what they have already done or what they already know instead of exploring new opportunities and ways of thinking or behaving.

- **Seeks Validation**
  Often relies on external approval to feel successful and struggles with self-doubt.

A Day in the Life of Lisa
Stuck in Her Ways

Lisa's day begins much like any other. She wakes up early, grabs a cup of coffee, and checks her emails mainly out of habit.

The morning's messages are a mix of order confirmations, questions from customers, and the usual marketing emails from brands she follows.

Among the emails is one from a digital marketing consultant offering a free masterclass on using social media to boost sales. Lisa glances at the subject line but quickly deletes it, thinking, "I don't have time for that."

Lisa starts her working day by packing orders. She has a small but loyal customer base that keeps her business just about afloat. As she prepares the packages, she is also mindlessly scrolling Instagram where she catches a glimpse of a competitor.

She notices their branded, eye-catching packaging and their engaging content. But rather than feeling inspired,

Thirteen *Making Bold Decisions*

Lisa feels annoyed.

"Why do they need to be so flashy? My customers like what I have just fine," she mutters to herself.

She dismisses the idea of updating her own packaging, or changing the way she approaches social media, instead viewing it as an unnecessary expense, a hassle, and a waste of time.

Lisa spends the next hour or so in 'faux action'. Busy for being busy sake but isn't actually doing anything that will propel her business forwards. She avoids looking at her latest products she launched months ago, they didn't perform well.

Instead of understanding why these items didn't sell as well as she thought they would, she writes them off as a bad idea, blaming the market for not catching on.

This pattern repeats often: when something doesn't work, it's easier for Lisa to blame external factors rather than to reflect on what she could do to improve.

As the morning progresses, Lisa reviews her sales numbers from the previous week. They're lower than she'd like, but instead of brainstorming ways to attract new customers and nurture the ones she's got, she sighs and blames the economy.

She decides to post a quick story on her Instagram account, a rare occurrence because she feels out of her depth with social media. The post is simple and uninspired: just a photo of her products with a meaningless caption and no call to action.

Thirteen Making Bold Decisions

She doesn't engage with her followers or respond to comments; she's too uncomfortable and uncertain of how to market herself effectively online.

Lisa's phone pings with a notification: a direct message from a customer suggesting that a product they bought isn't working well for them.

Instead of seeing this feedback as an opportunity for improvement or to understand how the customer was using the product, Lisa feels defensive and irritated.

"My products have been this way for years. Nobody else has this problem!" she thinks, dismissing the feedback without a second thought.

Lisa spends her afternoon scrolling through her competitors' websites and social media channels, feeling increasingly disheartened. She notices how they've embraced new and improved marketing strategies that help them get noticed and sell more products.

Deep down, she knows she should change, but the thought of learning new skills feels overwhelming. She convinces herself these trends are just fads and not worth her time.

Instead of working on her business, Lisa continues to busy herself with administrative tasks that feel safe and familiar. She organises her desk, and checks her inventory levels again, avoiding the hard work of actually strategising for growth.

When she thinks about the changes she could make, a wave of anxiety washes over her.

Thirteen *Making Bold Decisions*

"I'm too old for all this new stuff," she tells herself, reinforcing the belief that she can't keep up with younger, savvier business owners.

By the end of the day, Lisa feels drained. She hasn't made any real progress, and her to-do list is still full of tasks that could help her business grow if she'd just take action.

She sits down for dinner, but her mind is elsewhere, replaying the day's frustrations. She remembers an invitation from another small business owner to take part in a joint venture, but decides against it, worrying it'll be too much work with little reward.

As Lisa prepares to end her day, she checks her social media one last time and sees a post from a competitor announcing a successful new product launch. Instead of feeling motivated, Lisa feels defeated.

"They must have some secret I don't," she thinks, failing to recognise that her unwillingness to try new things is holding her back.

She puts her phone down, feeling overwhelmed and stuck, yet too paralysed by fear of the unknown to make a change.

Thirteen *Making Bold Decisions*

Stuck in the Cycle
Lisa's Mindset in Action

This version of Lisa's day-to-day actions are driven by a **fixed mindset** that keeps her stuck. She resists new opportunities, avoids challenges, and rejects feedback that could help her business evolve.

Lisa's routine is comfortable, but it's also the very thing keeping her stagnant. The fear of failure, the discomfort of learning new skills, and the reluctance to step outside her comfort zone are all barriers that prevent her from reaching her true potential.

Lisa's story serves as a powerful reminder: when you cling to what's familiar and refuse to adapt, your business can't grow.

Be honest with yourself, are you like Lisa? Are you holding onto outdated habits and beliefs, hoping the market will come back around to your way of doing things?

If so, it's time to embrace a **growth mindset**, take ownership of your actions, and step boldly into new opportunities that can elevate your business to new heights.

Growth Mindset
Embracing the Journey of Learning

A business owner with a growth mindset believes that abilities and intelligence can be developed through dedication and hard work.

Thirteen *Making Bold Decisions*

This mindset creates resilience, creativity, and a willingness to take on new challenges allowing their business to flourish.

Here are some common traits of a growth mindset and an example of what they look like in daily practice:

- **Embraces Challenges**
  Sees obstacles as opportunities to learn and improve.

- **Values Feedback**
  Encourages feedback from their customers knowing any criticism can be used as a tool for growth. Consistently looking for ways they can enhance their business.

- **Perseveres**
  Even when the going gets tough they don't give up easily; instead, they find a new way to overcome these obstacles to come out the other end with a better business as a result.

- **Takes Risks**
  Willing to try new things and take a chance on themselves by continuing to innovate, and explore uncharted territory.

- **Focuses On Learning**
  Prioritises personal and professional development by constantly finding ways to improve their knowledge.

Thirteen Making Bold Decisions

A Day in the Life of Lisa
The Evolving Entrepreneur

Lisa's alarm goes off early, but instead of dreading the day, she feels energised. She starts her morning with some exercise, listening to her favourite podcast about entrepreneurship and marketing trends.

As she exercises, she hears about a new social media trend that brands are using to engage customers. This immediately gives her ideas about how she could grow her own business.

After her run, Lisa makes a coffee and sits down at her desk. Her morning routine includes reviewing the analytics dashboard, which tracks website traffic, social media engagement, and sales performance.

Instead of just skimming the numbers, Lisa looks for patterns and opportunities for improvement. She notices one of her recent Instagram Reels, where she styled her newest collection, had significantly more engagement than her regular posts.

Excited, Lisa takes notes on what worked well in the Reel: perhaps it was the trending music, the behind-the-scenes glimpse, the hook she used or the quick styling tips that resonated with her audience.

She writes down ideas to create more content like this, always looking for ways to optimise what's working and most importantly, understanding why.

Lisa's next task is fulfilling customer orders, but she doesn't

Thirteen *Making Bold Decisions*

just pack and ship without thought. With each order, she includes a handwritten note thanking customers and a small card inviting them to leave feedback on their recent purchase. She's made it a habit to engage with her customers, valuing their input as a key component of her brand's growth.

After packing the orders, Lisa spends some time going live on social media, where she answers followers' questions about her business and products.

Today, a customer suggests a new colour for one of her best-selling jackets. Instead of dismissing the idea, Lisa adds it to a list of potential updates. She loves connecting with his customers and sees their feedback as invaluable data that can help refine her products and the service she offers.

Around lunchtime, Lisa schedules an hour to review her competitors. A new brand has recently entered the market, catching Lisa's attention with their marketing strategy.

Instead of feeling threatened, Lisa approaches this with curiosity. She spends time understanding their Instagram posts, noting how they engage with their followers and how they tell their brand story.

Lisa doesn't copy; she learns. She pulls up her own marketing plan and brainstorms ways to infuse some of these ideas into her brand while keeping true to her unique voice.

She decides to launch a series of Instagram Stories showing the sustainable sourcing process behind her

Thirteen Making Bold Decisions

fabrics, a nod to what's working for his competitor, but with a twist that highlights her own brand values.

Lisa's day isn't just about running the business; it's also about investing in her own growth. In the afternoon, she sets aside time to work on an online course about influencer marketing. It's not something she's fully comfortable with yet, but knows that mastering this skill could open up new avenues for her brand.

Lisa takes notes, asks questions, and even reaches out to other small business owners in the group to share insights and ideas.

When she finishes, Lisa immediately applies what she's learned by drafting an outreach email to a local influencer whose style aligns perfectly with her brand.

She doesn't worry about getting it perfect; instead focuses on taking action. Lisa understands every attempt, even the unsuccessful ones, is a learning experience that will help her improve.

As the day winds down, Lisa reviews her task list. She checks off what she's accomplished, but also takes time to reflect on what didn't go as planned.

One of her new products didn't sell as well as expected, so she dives into the data to understand why. Instead of feeling discouraged, Lisa views this as a puzzle to solve.

She sets a reminder to send out a survey to her customers to gather more insights on what they're looking for.

Before calling it a day, Lisa writes down her goals for

Thirteen *Making Bold Decisions*

tomorrow, making sure to include both routine tasks and new experiments she wants to try.

She knows growth doesn't come from doing the same thing every day: it comes from continually pushing the boundaries of what's comfortable.

Lisa's Mindset in Action
A Commitment to Growth

Lisa's approach to her business is now driven by a **growth mindset** that values learning, adapts to change, and seeks continuous improvement.

She views challenges as opportunities to learn and constantly asks herself:

"What can I do better?"

Lisa's willingness to experiment, accept feedback, and step outside her comfort zone keeps her brand evolving and customers engaged.

Unlike those stuck in a fixed mindset, Lisa doesn't fear competition; she sees it as a chance to sharpen and update her own strategy.

Reflect on Your Own Journey

Lisa's story is a testament to the power of a growth mindset. It's not about having all the answers; it's about being willing to find them. How can you start incorporating this mindset into your daily routine?

What actions can you take today that will set you up for success tomorrow?

Your business will only grow as much as you do.

Strategies to Shift from a Fixed to a Growth Mindset:

Re-frame Challenges as Learning Opportunities
Instead of seeing obstacles as roadblocks that simply can't be moved, view them as valuable lessons that will make you a better business owner.

> *Action Step:*
>
> - **Celebrate Progress, Not Just Results**
>   This reinforces your growth mindset and keeps you motivated. Every small step in the right direction is one that should be celebrated.
>
> - **Seek Feedback Actively**
>   Invite feedback from customers and mentors. Use it as a tool for growth, not as a measure of your worth.
>
> - **Adopt a 'Yet' Mentality**
>   When you catch yourself thinking, "I can't do this," add the word "yet." This simple shift opens the door to possibility and future growth.

Trust Your Expertise

You've invested time and energy into understanding your business, your products, and your market.

That knowledge is a powerful asset, lean into it!

Confidence comes from knowing your value and trusting you're equipped to make the right decisions.

Every successful business owner started somewhere.

They didn't have all the answers at first, but they trusted in their journey, adapted as they went and asked for help when they needed it.

You have that same potential.

Action Step:

- **Own Your Niche**
  Be the expert in your product category.
  The more knowledge you have, the more confident you'll be in your ability to stand out and the more value you will have to share with your perfect customers.

- **Highlight Past Wins**
  Reflect on your past successes, big or small. Whether it was a successful product launch, or a glowing customer review, these wins are evidence of your capability. Celebrate them and use them as fuel to keep moving forward.

Thirteen Making Bold Decisions

Embrace Calculated Risks

Building a successful business involves taking risks.

In fact you have already taken one of the biggest risks by starting your own business in the first place!

So, instead of seeing further risk as something to fear, approach it as an opportunity for growth.

Bold decisions are necessary to stand out, be noticed and get your products seen and sold.

Confidence will help you push past the fear of failure.

Some of the most successful businesses were built on bold moves, launching new products, entering new markets, or trying unconventional marketing strategies.

To be a true success you can't be a sheep and follow the crowd. Own your quirks, your uniqueness and put them front and centre.

You are your secret weapon! Nobody else has got you in their back pocket.

Risk isn't the enemy of success - inaction is.

Thirteen Making Bold Decisions

Action Step:

- **Start Small, Think Big**
  You don't have to take huge risks right away. Start with small, calculated decisions that push you slightly out of your comfort zone. Over time, these will build your risk tolerance and prepare you for bigger, bolder moves that will get you bigger, bolder results.

- **Experiment and Learn**
  Not every decision will lead to immediate success, and that's okay.
  The key is to treat every action as a learning experience. If something doesn't work out, understand why and what you could've done differently.
  Learn from it, and use that knowledge to make better decisions moving forward.

Make Decisions from a Place of Strength, Not Fear

Fear of failure or rejection can often hold business owners back from making bold decisions.

Acting from a place of fear limits your potential.

Confidence comes when you shift your mindset to make decisions from a place of **strength**, knowing that even if things don't go perfectly, you have the resilience and skills to navigate whatever comes next.

Thirteen Making Bold Decisions

Fear can paralyse you, but confidence allows you to step into your true power. When you make decisions from a place of strength, you're more likely to make choices that align with your long-term vision.

Action Step:

- **Use Affirmations**
  It might sound simple or a bit eccentric, but affirmations are a powerful tool for rewiring your mindset. Statements like, "I am capable of making bold decisions" or "I trust my instincts and abilities" can help you to have the confidence needed to act decisively.

- **Surround Yourself with Support**
  Confidence and the road to success isn't a solo journey. It is important to surround yourself with people who believe in your potential and can offer encouragement.
  Whether it's mentors, friends, or other business owners, having a support system can help you feel stronger in your decisions.

- **Focus on Solutions, Not Problems**
  When challenges arise, focus on finding solutions rather than dwelling on the problem.
  This shift in mindset makes you feel more in control and confident in your ability to handle whatever comes your way.

Thirteen *Making Bold Decisions*

Visualise Success

Visualisation is a powerful tool for not only boosting confidence but also setting yourself up for success.

When you can picture your desired outcome, it becomes easier to make bold moves to get there.

Olympic athletes often use visualisation to prepare for success. They see themselves crossing the finish line before they even start the race.

Action Step:

- **Daily Visualisation Practice**
  Spend a few minutes each morning visualising your perfect day and the outcomes you want to achieve. The clearer this vision becomes in your mind, the more confident you'll feel in making decisions that align with it.

- **Set Big Goals**
  Confidence grows when you work toward something significant. Set ambitious, yet achievable goals that push you out of your comfort zone. Chunk these big goals down into daily actions.

- **Focus on the Feeling**
  When visualising success, pay attention to how it feels. Imagine the pride, excitement, and fulfilment that comes with achieving your business goals. These positive emotions will help you to have the confidence to take bold steps in the right direction.

Commit to Continuous Growth

Confidence is not static: it's a muscle you must strengthen over time. The more you learn, evolve, and adapt, the more confident you'll become in your ability to make bold decisions.

Commit to the mindset that your growth is ongoing, and with each step forward, your confidence will expand.

Business isn't a straight line to success.

You will face setbacks, however every challenge is an opportunity to grow. Confidence isn't about avoiding failure; it's about knowing you can dust yourself off, learn from the experience and keep going.

Action Step:

- **Invest in Your Education**
  Whether it's through books like this, courses, or mentorship, continue learning.
  Knowledge is power.

- **Track Your Progress**
  Keep a journal of your achievements. Reflecting on how far you've come will remind you of your growth and boost your confidence when faced with new challenges.

- **Stay Curious**
  Confidence comes from being open to learning and adapting as you go.

Thirteen *Making Bold Decisions*

Wrapping Up

As we come to the end of this journey, it's time to reflect on everything you've discovered.

You now have a powerful set of strategies that will help get your products seen and sold, without burning yourself out.

You've explored methods to increase visibility, build customer loyalty, improve your service, and deliver value at every touchpoint.

But none of these strategies will be effective unless you have the confidence to implement them.

Remember, it's not about working harder, it's about working smarter.

By building your confidence, embracing bold decisions, and trusting in your ability to succeed, you can take your product business to the next level.

The journey doesn't end here, it's just the beginning!

You have the tools, the knowledge, and the confidence to make your business thrive.

**Now, go out there and
sell smarter, not harder!**

Thirteen *Making Bold Decisions*

Join The Zenith Training Program

Get expert support to start and grow your product business

Book your free discovery call today

About the Author

About the Author

My Mission Is Simple...

Regardless of what you sell,
or whether you have a physical or online location,
I believe every product based business can
flourish and grow, no matter the challenges.

With the right knowledge, tools, and a bit of inspiration,
you can achieve amazing results.

About the Author

I'm Samuel Chapman.

I'm living proof that success is not about where you start but how you rise.

Once a struggling salon owner buried in debt, I transformed my business into a thriving, award winning enterprise within two years.

Drawing on these insights, I went on to open a second salon, launch my own award winning product line, and become a coach and podcaster for product business owners worldwide.

My journey has been anything but ordinary. With years of experience running brick & mortar and online businesses along with a deep understanding of customer connection, marketing, and business operations, I know first-hand the challenges entrepreneurs face. But it's my passion for helping others combined with my proven strategies that truly sets me apart.

Through my coaching methodology, the Zenith Method, I empower product business owners to connect with their perfect customers, create irresistible offers without discounting, and build thriving businesses they love. I also host of The Abundant Business Podcast, where I share actionable advice, inspiring stories, and strategies to help entrepreneurs achieve lasting success.

About the Author

For more inspiration and insights...

visit
samuelchapman.com

follow me on Instagram
@productcoachsam

About the Author

Tune into
The Abundant Business Podcast

Apple   **Spotify**

www.ingramcontent.com/pod-product-compliance
Lightning Source LLC
Chambersburg PA
CBHW052156220526
45471CB00004B/1700